Imposs e

D0118175

Impossible Pie

A Cookbook of
Canadian Family Favourites

A Project for the
Hospital for Sick Children Capital Campaign

by

Recipes compiled by
Lucy Waverman

Canadian Cataloguing in Publication Data

Impossible Pie – a cookbook of Canadian family favourites

A project for the Hospital for Sick Children Capital Campaign.

ISBN 0-9694451-0-5

1. Cookery – Canada. I. Hospital for Sick Children.

TX715.6.I56 1990   641.5   C90-094967-8

Illustrations:
Katherine Brown/Ogilvy & Mather Advertising

Photographs:
Michael Shaw/Ashley and Crippen Photographers

Typesetting:
Quick Draw Graphics Ltd., Vancouver
(a division of The Printing House Ltd.)

Additional copies may be obtained by contacting:

The Printing House Fund Raising Office
15 Stanley Avenue
Toronto, Ontario M6J 1A4
(416) 363-5296

Printed in Canada

Contents

Acknowledgements

The following have donated their professional time and services. Without them, this book would not have been possible:

Ault Foods Limited

Katherine Brown/Ogilvy & Mather Advertising

Campbell Soup Company Ltd

Infocentre Network

Michael Shaw/Ashley and Crippen Photographers

The President's Choice Test Kitchen

Lucy Waverman

Thanks also to George Mitzithras, George's Gourmet Hot Dogs, Montcrest School, Clare Arfin and Marijke Zonnenfeld for recipe testing, and all the children who sat so patiently during the photographic sessions.

The Printing House Fund Raising Committee:

Janice O'Born, Chairperson; Lucy Waverman, Cookbook advisor; Edith Burch; Laird Saunderson; Valerie Fountain; Mara Teitelbaum

Together with a team of dedicated Printing House staff and families.

Contributors

The Printing House Fund Raising Committee would like to thank the following people who have generously submitted recipes. We regret that we were unable to include many recipes that were submitted, due to similarity or lack of space.

Martha Adams
Janet Ali
Colleen Allum
Olga Almeida
Berta Amaral
Naomi Amato
Teresa Armstrong
Elizabeth Baird
Fazia Baksh
Kathy Barratt
Angela Batt
Helen Bishop McDonald
Cathy Bolla
Sandra Bradley
Marilyn Brooks
Mary Brown
Edith Burch
Nancy Burch
Christina Burridge
Barbara Bush
Brian Calcafuoco
Gladys Campbell
Canada Pork Inc.
Canadian Living Test Kitchen
Barbara Caplan
Mr. and Mrs. Caplan
Debbie Carroll
Roni Chaleff
Penny Chapman
Mrs. Ethel Cherry
Simmie Clark
Sheila Clarke
Paola Scaravelli and Jon Cohen
E. Colville
Irene Cosman
Margit Cox

Kathleen Currie
Harold Cutler
Kim Daviau
Kathleen Davis
Marilyn Denis
Edith Downey
Linda Drtina
Marcela Drtina-Rocha
Jill Edwardson
Mrs. J. Ellison
Robbie Evans
Sharon Evans
Audrey Eyre
Jodi Feldman
Monique Fernandez
Beryl Fleming
Ms. J. Fleming
Gerry Forbes
Forest Manor Public School
Maureen Forrester
Valerie Fountain
Margaret Fraser
Barbara Frum
Trudy Gelber
Kathleen Gibson
Real Goodman
Mary Lou Gossage
Joanne Gougeon
Wayne Gretzky
Mike and Carol Hall
June Harding
Cheryl Heeney
Brandy Hermant
Karen Herring
Barb Holland
Lorraine Horne

Lois Hughes
Catherine Hugill
Peggy Hutchison
Norman Jewison
Shirley Johnston
Mr. and Mrs. Jolson
Nicole Joly
Janet Judd
Karen Kain
Marion Kane
Hartley Kell
Nancy Kennedy
Gary Kirshenbaum
Ruth Kirshner
Olga Kuch
A. Leppanen
Denise Lewis
Diane Lewis
Laya Liberman
Honey Lieberman
Anne Lindsay
Marilyn Linton
Leya Ludwig
Linda Lundstrom
Laura MacDonald
Nancy MacDonnell
Leon Major
Peter Mansbridge
Mr. and Mrs. McBride
Ms. M. McCabe
Gayle McCaig
Christina McCall
Don McCarthy
Mary McGrath
Margo McKirdy
Carol McKnight
Barbara McQuade
Wendy Mesley
Mary Meyers
Ed Mirvish
Mono Cliffs Inn

Catherine Morrissey
Mila Mulroney
Anne Murray
Christine Nagy
Melissa Napier-Andrews
Agnes Nazar
Jay Nelson
Rita Nelson
Mary Nesbitt
New Zealand Lamb Co. Ltd.
Janice O'Born
Ontario Crafts Council –
   Northern Region
Patty Perry
R.B. Peterson Family
Shelley Peterson
Heidi Proctor
Jill Reilly
Sandie Rinaldo
Anne Roberts
Janet Rodger
Trent Rowe
Janet Rowley
Ms. Ruscoe
Alicia Russell
Joanna Sable
Myra Sable
Lila Satok
Laird Saunderson
Judy Schachter
Madeline Schmidt
Brenda Schopp
Rosie Schwartz
Margaret Scott-Atkinson
Doreen Sears
Rosemary Sexton
Sharon, Lois and Bram
Rosalie Sharp
Merelyn Shore
Ann M. Skov
Carol Smith

Chris Smith-Collins
Kristina Spence
Estelle Steinhauer
Bonnie Stern
Deborah L. Stewart
Dorothy Stothart
Jackie Sullivan
Ladka Sweeney
Irma Tassy
Ethel Teitelbaum
Mara Teitelbaum
Sari Teitelbaum
Veronica Tennant
The Globe Restaurant
Paul Tichauer
Maureen Tingley

Joyce Trimmer
Sally Venor
Janis Vodden
Margot Waugh
Lucy Waverman
Sara Waxman
Marlene Weeden
Hilary Weston
Carol White
V. Whitefield
Cynthia Wine
Judi Winston
Gladys Joy Wiseman
David Wood
Rochelle Zastrau

Preface

Two years ago, *Impossible Pie* seemed an impossible dream. I had already been active in fund-raising drives and knew how difficult it could be to raise needed capital, no matter how noble the cause. And in this case the cause is, I believe, one of the most deserving – financial support of the new Hospital for Sick Children building.

My husband, Earle, and I talked of several ways to raise money, but none of them seemed likely to succeed. It was Earle who proposed the idea of a cookbook. I was sceptical at first, knowing how many cookbooks line the shelves of bookstores and libraries. But the more we examined the notion, the more appealing it became. So in the spring of 1988, a small team of dedicated volunteers started to put this important fund-raising project into high gear. We decided our cookbook would not be a large, lavishly illustrated volume, more at home gracing coffee tables instead of kitchen counters. Nor would it deal with recipes that rely on artificial additives. What we wanted was an honest cookbook – a compendium of "back-to-basics" recipes that reflected simple virtues and the culinary traditions of families that have been passed from generation to generation.

Through advertisements and other promotions, we solicited recipes. We were thrilled by the response. More than two thousand recipes were sent in by contributors across the country, including many celebrities and professional cooks who took the time to support this worthy cause. From these, cookbook author and food expert Lucy Waverman narrowed the field, and these recipes were submitted to the test kitchens of the Campbell Soup Company Ltd and The President's Choice Test Kitchen, who generously donated their services. Our final selection of almost two hundred recipes are the subject of *Impossible Pie.*

As the chairperson of this fund-raising mission, I have been fortunate to work with a group of people who have been unwavering in their commitment to the project and entirely selfless in donating their time – often well into the night – and their considerable talents. They have my deepest gratitude.

All of us who have laboured on *Impossible Pie* feel a sense of pride and accomplishment in bringing the book to market. **The entire proceeds generated by sales will be donated** to the Hospital for Sick Children Capital Campaign. In purchasing this book, you are supporting one of the most important and valuable medical facilities in the world.

Janice O'Born
July, 1990

Foreword

When I was growing up, having dinner together as a family was a very important part of my life. My mother cooked good, nourishing meals and didn't try to feed us food she knew we'd reject, so mealtimes were pleasurable and gave us an opportunity to talk about everyday events and discuss decisions that had to be made. It was our time for keeping in touch.

Eating together as a family has gone out of fashion over the years, mainly because both parents have become breadwinners and don't have time to cook. But now in the Nineties, people are once again expressing the desire for these past values, and eating together is coming back into vogue.

This book is dedicated to all of you who want to be back in the kitchen, and enjoy it. From the many recipes submitted by cooks from all over Canada, I have chosen nearly two hundred that, to me, represent the best of family cooking – tasty, wholesome recipes with easy-to-find ingredients that are suitable for families to cook and eat together. The recipes are simple to make, they have all been professionally tested, and they are geared to the tastes of kids as well as adults.

I hope you enjoy using this book as much as I have enjoyed helping to coordinate it. I know it will become a standard in your kitchen.

Lucy Waverman
July, 1990

Introduction

Feeding children can be a challenge at the best of times, despite parents' valiant efforts to provide a nourishing and varied diet.

Canada's Food Guide has traditionally been used as the basis of sound nutrition, and choosing a variety of foods from its four main groups – milk and milk products; fruits and vegetables; breads and cereals; meat, fish, poultry and alternatives – will ensure adequate nutrition for you and your family. The new recommendations from Health and Welfare Canada focus increasingly on the importance of complex carbohydrates, such as whole grains, legumes and starchy vegetables, which are high in fibre. So it's a good idea to try to include baked goods using whole grains, and legume or grain-based salads or dips that are relatively low in saturated fats and sugars.

Too many parents try to force their child to eat. But children usually know when and how much food they need, and their appetites can be influenced by many factors such as amount of sleep and exercise, and rate of growth. Many children have growth spurts around the ages of two months, ten months, twelve months and five years. A poor appetite with weight loss may well indicate illness.

Between-meal snacks can discourage a child's appetite at meal times, but snacks are not necessarily a bad thing. Younger children especially tend to eat smaller meals and rely on snacks to supplement their meals. Give them nutritious choices such as crackers and cheese or peanut butter, bran muffins, yogurt, fresh fruit and vegetables. Don't worry too much if their snacking habits are healthy, but do try to establish a fairly routine eating pattern, even if this consists of three meals and three snacks a day, rather than allowing constant snacking, which could predispose a child to obesity later on.

Try to encourage your child to have a positive attitude towards good food. Let your children help you with shopping and food preparation – taking part in the creation of a meal always makes it more appealing. Praise your children for their help, and for trying new foods. Try to introduce dishes with a variety of colours, textures and flavours, and let young children handle and explore their food (wearing clothes and bibs that can be easily washed!). Provide child-sized utensils and cups. Most important, remember that your own attitude towards food and eating will influence your children.

One note of caution. Avoid giving young children foods that are small and round and can easily lodge in the windpipe. Hot dogs, grapes, popcorn, nuts, hard candies and raw vegetables such as carrots can accidentally be inhaled. They should only be offered under close supervision and should never be given to a child who is running around rather than sitting down.

We hope that you and your family will try some of the recipes in this book – family favourites that have been chosen because they are easy to make, nutritious and have stood the test of time – and that they will help you to make mealtimes in your home enjoyable, as well as healthful.

Elena Randall, R.P.Dt.
Assistant Director,
Food Services
Hospital for Sick Children

Anne Dumas, R.P.Dt.
Assistant Director,
Nutrition Services
Hospital for Sick Children

1
Appetizers & Soups

Sara Waxman's Sticky Walnuts

Sara Waxman places bowls of these spicy walnuts around the room at a party. She deep-fries them, but we bake them to reduce the fat. The walnuts can be made in advance and stored in a tightly covered container. You can also use other nuts in this recipe.

1 lb	walnut halves	500 g
1 cup	granulated sugar	250 mL
1 tbsp	five-spice powder	15 mL
	Salt to taste	

Five-spice powder is a powerful combination of ground anise, fennel, cloves, cinnamon and ginger. If you don't have it, use a mixture of equal parts cinnamon, ginger, cloves and a pinch of nutmeg.

1. Preheat oven to 350° F (180° C).

2. Place walnuts in a saucepan and add water just to cover. Heat to boiling, then boil for 1 minute, stirring occasionally. Drain and pat dry.

3. Meanwhile, in a small bowl, combine sugar and five-spice powder.

4. While still warm, place walnuts in a bowl. Sprinkle sugar/spice mixture over the walnuts and toss to coat them thoroughly.

5. Spread walnuts on an oiled baking sheet. Bake for 20 minutes, stirring occasionally, or until sugar caramelizes. Cool completely and sprinkle with salt.

Makes 1 lb (500 g)

Pizza

Make this basic pizza, or spread toppings of your choice on the cheese before baking (this prevents the cheese from drying out!). You can try other cheeses, such as fontina or goat cheese, instead of the mozzarella.

SUGGESTED PIZZA TOPPINGS:
- sautéed mushrooms
- sliced pepperoni
- sautéed onions
- sliced tomatoes
- sliced and pitted black olives
- sautéed sliced sweet peppers
- pineapple chunks
- chopped anchovies
- any cooked vegetable
- herbs such as basil, oregano and rosemary

1	package dry yeast (1 tbsp/15 mL)	1
1 cup	lukewarm water	250 mL
1 tsp	granulated sugar	5 mL
1 tsp	salt	5 mL
1/4 cup	olive oil	50 mL
2-1/2 cups	all-purpose flour	625 mL
1 cup	tomato sauce	250 mL
1 cup	grated mozzarella cheese	250 mL

1. Preheat oven to 400° F (200 C°).

2. In a large bowl, combine yeast, water and sugar. Let sit for 10 minutes. Add salt, oil and 1-1/2 cups (375 mL) flour. Mix well. Add remaining flour. Knead together until mixture becomes elastic. Roll out and fit into a 12-inch (30 cm) pizza pan.

3. Spread sauce on dough; sprinkle on cheese.

4. Bake for 20 to 25 minutes, or until dough is browned and cheese bubbles.

Serves 4

Taco Pie

You control the amount of zing by your choice of salsa. This dish is a favourite at outdoor barbecues or as a nutritious snack any time. Serve it with a bowl of taco or tortilla chips for munching.

1/2 cup	cottage cheese	125 mL
8 oz	cream cheese, at room temperature	250 g
1 cup	salsa	250 mL
1/2 cup	chopped green onion	125 mL
1/3 cup	finely shredded lettuce	75 mL
2	large tomatoes, chopped	2
1-1/2 cups	grated Cheddar cheese	375 mL

1. In a bowl, cream together cottage cheese and cream cheese. Spread on bottom of glass pie dish. Spread on salsa and sprinkle with remaining ingredients.

Serves 6

HOMEMADE SALSA
In a skillet, heat 1 tbsp (15 mL) olive oil. Add 1 chopped onion, 1 chopped clove garlic, 3 chopped tomatoes, 1/2 tsp (2 mL) dried oregano and 1 chopped fresh green chili. Season with salt and pepper to taste, and a pinch of sugar. Cook gently for 15 minutes. Makes about 1 cup (250 mL).

Margaret Fraser's Pepper-Crusted Pork Tenderloin Slices

Pork tenderloin is the leanest cut of pork with little fat. Spareribs have 44 grams of fat per 4 oz/125 g serving as compared to pork tenderloin which has 14 grams of fat per 4 oz/125 g serving.

Grilled pork tenderloin slices, warm or at room temperature, make an unusual appetizer when served with the sour cream dipping sauce. This can also be served with rice as a main course.

3	pork tenderloins (about 12 oz/375 g each)	3
1/2 cup	mango chutney	125 mL
3 tbsp	coarsely ground black pepper	45 mL

Mango Sauce

1/2 cup	sour cream	125 mL
1/3 cup	mango chutney	75 mL

1. Preheat oven to 375° F (190° C), or ready coals in barbecue.

2. Wipe tenderloins with damp cloth and place on sheet of waxed paper. Spread 1/4 cup (50 mL) of chutney over one side of tenderloins. Sprinkle half of the pepper over tenderloins and turn them over. Spread remaining 1/4 cup (50 mL) chutney over tenderloins; sprinkle with remaining pepper.

3. Grill tenderloins on lightly greased grill over medium-hot coals for about 10 minutes per side, or until meat thermometer inserted in thickest part of meat registers 175° F (80° C). Alternatively, place tenderloins in greased baking dish. Roast in oven for 20 minutes; turn and roast for 20 to 30 minutes longer, or until meat thermometer registers 175° F (80° C). Cool slightly and carve into 3/4-inch (2 cm) thick slices of tenderloin.

4. In a bowl, blend together sour cream and chutney. Serve as dipping sauce.

Serves 8 to 12

Brie Strata

A great appetizer or brunch dish, this strata puffs up like a soufflé. Use any leftover cheeses if you wish. This recipe can be assembled the night before serving; refrigerate until 30 minutes before baking. Serve it topped with fruit salsa.

1/2 cup	butter	125 mL
8 to 10	slices white bread, crusts removed	8 to 10
4	eggs	4
1-1/2 cups	milk	375 mL
1/2 tsp	salt	2 mL
1/2 tsp	pepper	2 mL
12 oz	Brie cheese, rind removed	375 g
1/2 tsp	paprika	2 mL

1. Butter one side of bread slices.

2. In a large bowl, beat eggs and whisk together with milk, salt and pepper.

3. Cut Brie into cubes.

4. Place half the bread slices, buttered side up, in a greased 9-inch (2.5 L) square baking dish. Top with half of the Brie. Repeat with remaining bread and Brie. Pour milk/egg mixture over bread. Sprinkle with paprika. Let stand for at least 30 minutes before baking.

5. Preheat oven to 350° F (180° C).

6. Bake for 35 to 40 minutes or until puffed and browned. To serve, cut strata into squares and top with fruit salsa.

Serves 6

FRUIT SALSA
This sauce can also be served with ice cream, pancakes or crêpes. In a large bowl, combine 2 cups (500 mL) diced fresh strawberries, 1 diced pear, 1 tbsp (15 mL) honey and 1 tbsp (15 mL) lime juice. Serve at room temperature. Makes 2 cups (500 mL).

Quick Salmon Mousse

A light, savoury salmon mousse that does double duty as a stuffing for raw vegetables or a dip, from the Fisheries Council of British Columbia. When made with light sour cream and mayonnaise, this mousse contains only 545 calories per cup.

When you use canned salmon, leave the bones and skin in, as they contain calcium (the bones in one 7-1/2-oz/ 213 g can of salmon contains more calcium than an 8-oz (250 g) glass of milk).

1	7-1/2 oz (213 g) Pacific salmon, drained	1
2 tbsp	sour cream	25 mL
2 tbsp	mayonnaise	25 mL
2 tsp	lemon juice	10 mL
1/4 tsp	Worcestershire sauce	1 mL
dash	Tabasco sauce	
2 tbsp	minced green onions or fresh coriander	25 mL

1. In a food processor fitted with the steel blade, process salmon until smooth. Add sour cream, mayonnaise, lemon juice, Worcestershire and Tabasco. Process for 30 seconds.

2. Serve as a dip, or spoon or pipe into fresh mushroom caps, Belgian endive spears or hollowed-out cherry tomatoes. Sprinkle with minced green onions or coriander.

**Makes about 1 cup (250 mL),
enough for 40 medium mushroom caps**

Mushroom and Shrimp Appetizer

This recipe is from Peggy Hutchison, Vice-President of Patient Services at the Hospital for Sick Children. She serves this as a nibbly before dinner. It can be made the day before serving.

Marinating your food in an aromatic mixture helps to soften the fibres of meat and fish while adding flavour to the food.

3 tbsp	olive oil	45 mL
1 tbsp	wine vinegar	15 mL
12	large shrimp, cooked	12
12	large mushroom caps	12
1 tbsp	butter	15 mL
2 tbsp	lemon juice	25 mL
1/4 cup	sliced pimento	50 mL
4 oz	cream cheese, at room temperature	125 g
	Salt and pepper to taste	
2 tbsp	chopped parsley	25 mL

1. In a bowl, combine olive oil and vinegar. Add shrimp, toss and marinate mixture for 1 hour.

2. In a skillet, simmer mushroom caps in butter and lemon juice for 3 minutes, turning once. Place upside-down on a rack and allow to drain very well.

3. Reserve 12 pimento slices for garnishing and finely chop the rest. In a bowl, combine pimentos, cream cheese, salt and pepper. Spoon into mushroom caps.

4. Drain the shrimp and place on top of the cheese mixture. Garnish with the parsley and a slice of the remaining pimento. Refrigerate until serving.

Serves 6

Peter Mansbridge's Crabmeat and Avocado

Peter Mansbridge of The National *makes this appetizer for special dinners.*

Children will enjoy growing an avocado plant from the leftover pit. Stick three toothpicks around the middle of an avocado pit. Balance the toothpicks on the rim of a glass filled with water, so that the rounded end of the pit sits in the water. Check daily to make sure the water level is maintained.

1	5-oz (142 g) can snow crabmeat	1
4	green onions, chopped	4
1 tbsp	lemon juice	15 mL
1 tbsp	mayonnaise	15 mL
	Salt and pepper to taste	
1	ripe avocado	1

1. Drain crabmeat well. In a bowl, combine crabmeat, green onions, lemon juice and mayonnaise. Season well. Mix gently just to combine.

2. Split avocado, discard pit and fill hollows to overflowing with crabmeat mixture. Serve immediately.

Serves 2

Weight Conversions

1 pound = 454 grams	1 kilo = 2.24 lbs
8 ounces = 227 grams	500 grams = 1.12 lbs
4 ounces = 113 grams	250 grams = 0.56 lbs
1 ounce = 28 grams	100 grams = 3.5 oz

Bonnie Stern's Hummus with Sesame

From Bonnie Stern's Appetizers *published by Random House. Bonnie serves this appetizer with sesame crackers, pita chips, vegetable slices, black bread or tortilla chips.*

Fresh coriander is also called cilantro or Chinese parsley. It has a fragrant taste and smell and is an indigenous ingredient of Mexican, Southeast Asian and Indian cooking. If you can't find it, use fresh parsley. Dried ground coriander is not a substitute for fresh coriander.

1	19-oz (540 mL) can chickpeas	1
2	cloves garlic, minced	2
3 tbsp	lemon juice	45 mL
3 tbsp	olive oil	45 mL
1/2 tsp	Tabasco sauce	2 mL
1/2 tsp	oriental sesame oil	2 mL
1/2 tsp	ground cumin	2 mL
2 tbsp	chopped fresh coriander	25 mL
	Lemon slices	

1. Place chickpeas in a food processor fitted with the steel blade. Purée coarsely. (If you are using a blender, add 1/4 cup/50 mL water and purée in two batches).

2. Add garlic, lemon juice, olive oil, Tabasco, sesame oil and cumin. Purée until as smooth as you wish.

3. Transfer to a serving bowl. Sprinkle with coriander and decorate with lemon slices.

Makes about 1-1/2 cups (375 mL)

Salmon-Stuffed Eggs

A great appetizer or brunch dish, with canned salmon blended into a zesty sauce and served over hard-cooked eggs, topped with caviar.

Red caviar is the slightly salted eggs of salmon; black caviar comes from sturgeon, and is much more expensive than salmon caviar. It is produced in both the U.S.S.R. and Iran. Canada produces excellent-quality salmon caviar.

1	7-1/2-oz (213 g) can Pacific salmon	1
1 tsp	butter	5 mL
1/3 cup	finely chopped onion	75 mL
1-1/2 tsp	curry powder	7 mL
1	bay leaf	1
2 tsp	lemon juice	10 mL
1 cup	mayonnaise	250 mL
2 tsp	mango chutney	10 mL
2 tbsp	whipping cream	25 mL
12	hard-cooked eggs, shelled	12
	Alfalfa sprouts and salmon caviar for garnish	

1. Drain salmon juices and reserve juices.

2. In a skillet, heat butter. Sauté onion until tender. Add curry powder and cook for 2 minutes. Add salmon juices, bay leaf and lemon juice. Simmer, uncovered, for 5 minutes over low heat. Cool.

3. Remove bay leaf and transfer mixture to a food processor together with salmon, mayonnaise, chutney and cream. Process until smooth. Cover and refrigerate for several hours or overnight.

4. Just prior to serving, carefully cut eggs in half. Spoon some of the sauce over the eggs and serve garnished with alfalfa sprouts and salmon caviar.

Serves 12

Ginger Carrot Soup

This is a favourite at the Globe Restaurant, a fine country restaurant in Rosemont, on Highway 89, just one hour north of Toronto.

3 tbsp	butter	45 mL
3/4 cup	finely chopped onion	175 mL
1/4 cup	finely chopped ginger root	50 mL
1/4 cup	all-purpose flour	50 mL
6 cups	chicken stock	1.5 L
1-1/2 lb	carrots, peeled and sliced	750 g
1 tsp	granulated sugar	5 mL
1-1/2 cups	light cream	375 mL
1/4 tsp	cinnamon	1 mL
	Salt and pepper to taste	
1	raw carrot cut into julienne strips	1

When buying fresh ginger, look for a smooth, firm root. Peel the skin off with a small knife. Don't store ginger in the refrigerator, as the dampness makes it go mouldy; instead, store the root, uncovered, in a cupboard.

1. In a large saucepan, melt butter over medium heat. Add onions and ginger root; cook, stirring, until onion becomes translucent.

2. Add flour, mix and cook for 1 minute.

3. Add stock, carrots and sugar. Bring to a boil. Simmer, covered, until the carrots are cooked, approximately 15 minutes.

4. In a blender or a food processor fitted with the steel blade, purée mixture in batches.

5. Return soup to the saucepan. Stir in cream and cook over low heat, stirring occasionally, until hot.

6. Add cinnamon and salt and pepper to taste. Simmer for 5 minutes. Pour into a heated tureen and garnish with julienned carrot.

Serves 6 to 8

Blueberry Soup

Fruit soups are delightful served before a summer barbecue.
Serve them in chilled glass mugs.

Picking fresh blueberries is a great summer activity. Children will be anxious to try this soup after having helped in picking the berries.

1	10-oz (284 g) package frozen unsweetened defrosted blueberries or 2 cups (500 mL) fresh blueberries	1
1-1/2 cups	water	375 mL
1/2 cup	granulated sugar	125 mL
2 tbsp	orange juice	25 mL
1/2 tsp	grated orange rind	2 mL
2 cups	blueberry yogurt	500 mL
4	thin orange slices	4

1. Reserve a few blueberries for garnish. In a large saucepan, combine remaining blueberries, water, sugar, orange juice and rind. Mix well and bring to a boil. Reduce heat, cover and simmer for 20 minutes.

2. Sieve soup through a strainer. Chill.

3. Stir in yogurt. Serve icy cold. Over each portion float an orange slice topped with the reserved blueberries.

Serves 4 to 6

Barb Holland's Winter Vegetable and Lentil Soup

A hearty, colourful main-dish soup that's chock full of vegetables, from microwave expert Barb Holland. Serve with whole wheat rolls.

1/2 cup	dried green lentils, rinsed	125 mL
2 tbsp	butter	25 mL
1	onion, cut in half and thinly sliced	1
1	clove garlic, minced	1
2 cups	shredded cabbage	500 mL
3	small carrots, thinly sliced	3
1	stalk celery, sliced	1
2 cups	beef stock	500 mL
1	19-oz (540 mL) can tomatoes, undrained	1
1 tsp	salt	5 mL
1/2 tsp	dried basil	2 mL
1/2 tsp	dried thyme	2 mL
1/4 tsp	pepper	1 mL
1/4 tsp	granulated sugar	1 mL

1. In a small saucepan, cover lentils with 1 cup (250 mL) cold water. Bring to a boil, reduce heat and simmer, covered, for 20 to 25 minutes, or until almost tender. Drain.

2. In a large saucepan, heat butter over medium heat. Sauté vegetables until softened. Add remaining ingredients, including lentils, cover and bring to a boil. Reduce heat and simmer for 30 to 40 minutes, or until vegetables and lentils are tender. Serve immediately.

Serves 8

You can buy both red (brown) and green lentils. The green lentils have more flavour and texture than the red ones, which don't have an outer seed coat. Red lentils cook to a purée; green lentils tend to stay whole. Lentils are very nutritious and are often used as a protein substitute.

MICROWAVE METHOD
Place lentils in a 6-cup (1.5 L) microwavable dish and cover with 1 cup (250 mL) hot water. Cover and microwave at High (100%) for 3 to 4 minutes, or until boiling. Microwave at Medium-Low (30%) for 15 to 25 minutes, or until lentils are tender. Let stand for 5 minutes, then drain.

Combine butter, onion, garlic, cabbage, carrots and celery in an 8-cup (2 L) microwavable dish. Cover and microwave at High (100%) for 6 to 8 minutes, or until vegetables are softened. Stir partway through cooking.

Stir in remaining ingredients and lentils. Cover and microwave at High (100%) for 10 to 12 minutes, or until vegetables and lentils are very tender. Let stand for a few minutes before serving.

Tomato Apple Celery Soup

*Combined with fresh bread and cheese, this soup makes a
wonderful autumn supper. If you use a food processor,
you do not have to sieve the soup.*

Use a cooking apple in soups, for a tart flavour. The best apples for cooking are Northern Spies, Granny Smiths or Mutsus.

1/4 cup	butter	50 mL
2 cups	finely chopped onions	500 mL
6	tomatoes, unpeeled, cored and chopped	6
3	apples, unpeeled, cored and chopped	3
2-1/2 cups	chopped celery	625 mL
4 cups	chicken stock	1 L
1/2 cup	whipping cream	125 mL
	Chopped chives	

1. In a heavy large saucepan, melt butter. Sauté onions until golden, about 2 minutes. Add tomatoes, apples, celery and stock. Cover and simmer for 30 minutes. Stir often.

2. Purée soup in a food processor or blender and sieve. Return to saucepan and gently reheat for 20 minutes on low heat.

3. In bowl, whip cream. Serve soup topped with a dollop of whipped cream and chives.

Serves 10 to 12

Cream of Mushroom Soup

1/3 cup	butter	75 mL
1 lb	mushrooms, sliced	500 g
1	small onion, finely chopped	1
2 tsp	all-purpose flour	10 mL
3 cups	chicken stock	750 mL
1 cup	whipping cream	250 mL
	Salt and pepper to taste	
2 tbsp	chopped parsley	25 mL

When buying mushrooms, look for firm heads with closed gills underneath. Never wash mushrooms, because they will absorb the water. Instead, wipe them clean with a soft brush or cloth.

1. In a large saucepan, melt butter over medium heat. Cook mushrooms for 5 minutes. Remove mushrooms and set aside.

2. In remaining liquid in saucepan, cook chopped onions for 10 minutes.

3. Add flour and cook for 1 minute. Gradually add chicken stock, whisking continuously. Add half of the reserved mushrooms. Simmer for 5 minutes.

4. Purée mixture in a food processor until smooth. Return soup to saucepan. Stir in cream and remaining mushrooms. Season with salt and pepper. Sprinkle with chopped parsley.

Serves 6 to 8

Carrot Pumpkin Soup

This unusual first course soup is especially nice for a formal dinner.

Don't try to cook with your Halloween pumpkins, as they are too stringy. But children will enjoy baking the pumpkin seeds for munching. Wash the seeds, rubbing off any pulp. Spread them on a baking sheet and sprinkle with salt. Bake at 250° F (120° C) for 20 to 30 minutes, or until slightly browned.

1 tbsp	butter	15 mL
1	large onion, sliced	1
1	clove garlic, chopped	1
1 lb	carrots, sliced	500 g
1 cup	pumpkin	250 mL
1 cup	drained canned tomatoes	250 mL
5 cups	chicken stock	1.25 L
1/2 cup	orange juice	125 mL
1/2 tsp	salt	2 mL
pinch	dried basil	pinch
1 tsp	chopped fresh mint, or 1/2 tsp (2 mL) dried	5 mL
	Pepper to taste	
1/2 cup	whipped cream (optional)	125 mL
	Chopped chives (optional)	

1. In a large saucepan, melt butter on medium heat. Add the onion and garlic and cook until very tender. Add carrots, pumpkin, tomatoes, stock, orange juice, salt and basil.

2. Bring to a boil. Reduce heat and simmer, covered, for 30 minutes, or until vegetables are very tender.

3. In a food processor or blender, blend mixture until smooth.

4. Return soup to saucepan. Add mint and pepper. Cook until heated through.

5. In bowl, whip cream. Serve soup topped with a dollop of whipped cream and sprinkle of chives.

Serves 8

Split Pea Soup

*You could add 1 cup (250 mL) diced smoked ham
with the vegetables for a heartier soup.*

2/3 cup	dried split green peas	150 mL
1/3 cup	butter	75 mL
1	small onion, finely chopped	1
1	leek (white part only), finely chopped	1
1	small carrot, diced	1
3	potatoes, peeled and diced	3
3 cups	chicken stock	750 mL
	Salt and pepper to taste	

Dried peas can be yellow or green. Split dried peas are simply whole peas that have been cut in half. Unlike whole peas, split peas do not have to be soaked before cooking.

1. Wash dried peas. Place peas in a large saucepan with 6 cups (1.5 L) water. Bring to a boil and boil for 5 minutes. Remove from heat and let stand for 2 hours. Drain. Cover peas with 6 cups (1.5 L) of fresh water.

2. Bring peas to a boil and simmer, covered, for approximately 45 minutes, or until tender. Drain.

3. In a separate large saucepan, melt butter. Add onion, leek, carrot and potatoes. Saute for 10 minutes. Stir in stock and peas. Cook, covered, for 1 hour.

4. In a blender or food processor, blend mixture a cup at a time, and then return to saucepan. Thin with more stock if needed. Season with salt and pepper.

Serves 6

Spinach and Green Pea Soup

From The Total Fibre Book *by Helen Bishop-McDonald and Margaret Fraser (Grosvenor Press), this soup is full of fibre and low in fat. For a thinner soup, add 1 cup (250 mL) milk.*

1 tbsp	butter	15 mL
2	leeks (white parts only), sliced	2
2 cups	fresh or frozen peas	500 mL
2 cups	packed torn fresh spinach	500 mL
2 cups	chicken stock	500 mL
1/4 tsp	dried savory	1 mL
	Salt and pepper to taste	
	Plain yogurt (optional)	

1. In a saucepan, melt butter over medium heat. Cook leeks, covered, until soft and fragrant but not browned.

2. Add peas, spinach, chicken stock and savory. Bring to a boil, reduce heat, cover and simmer for 20 minutes.

3. In a food processor or blender, purée soup in batches until smooth. Season with salt and pepper to taste.

4. Serve with a drizzle of yogurt on top of each serving, if desired.

Serves 4

To prepare leeks for cooking, cut off the top dark-green leaves (use only the light-green and white parts). With a knife, split the leek lengthwise down to the root. Wash under cold running water, separating the layers gently until all the dirt is dislodged.

Vichyssoise

Vichyssoise is not a French invention. It was invented in the early 1900s by a New York chef who was looking for a cold soup to serve before an elegant dinner.

1/4 cup	butter	50 mL
1 cup	diced onions	250 mL
2	leeks, diced	2
2	potatoes, peeled and diced	2
3 cups	chicken stock	750 mL
1/4 tsp	pepper	1 mL
3 tbsp	plain yogurt	45 mL
1 cup	light cream	250 mL
	Salt and pepper to taste	
2 tbsp	chopped parsley	25 mL

Homemade chicken stock is easy to make and has a much lower salt content. Freeze homemade stock in ice cube trays for easy use in sauces, gravies and stir-fries.

1. In a large saucepan, melt butter on medium heat. Sauté onions and leeks until golden-brown. Add potatoes, stock and pepper.

2. Cover and bring to a boil, then reduce heat and let simmer for 15 to 20 minutes, or until potatoes are cooked.

3. In a blender or food processor, purée mixture. Refrigerate.

4. Before serving, add the yogurt and cream, mixing very well. Add salt and pepper to taste. Sprinkle parsley on the individual servings.

Serves 6

Carol White's Pasta and Bean Soup (Pasta E Fagioli)

Carol White's hearty dish never fails to get rave reviews. "I originally started making it as a soup (from an excellent Bonnie Stern recipe), but over the years it has evolved into a thick stew that my family calls the ultimate comfort food." An Italian cook shared the tip about adding the Parmesan cheese rind – it adds a wonderful rich flavour. This is one of the few dishes that benefits from whole wheat pasta. Serve with crusty bread and a rustic Italian red wine. Follow with a mixed green salad.

3 tbsp	olive oil	45 mL
5	cloves garlic, finely chopped	5
2	large onions, chopped	2
6	carrots, sliced	6
1/2 tsp	hot red chili flakes (or more to taste)	2 mL
	Rind of a wedge of Parmigiano Reggiano (optional)	
6 cups	chicken stock	1.5 L
2	28-oz (796 mL) cans plum tomatoes, undrained	2
3	19-oz (540 mL) cans kidney beans, drained and rinsed	3
2	10-oz (550 mL) cans chickpeas, drained and rinsed	2
12 oz	whole wheat macaroni or other small pasta	375 g
	Salt and pepper to taste	
1/2 cup	grated Parmesan cheese	125 mL

1. In a large saucepan, heat oil. Add garlic, onions, carrots and chili flakes and cook, stirring, until tender; do not brown. If you have the rind from a wedge of Parmesan cheese, add it to the saucepan and stir well.

2. Add chicken stock and tomatoes with their liquid; break up tomatoes with the back of a spoon. Bring to a boil, reduce heat, partially cover and simmer for 30 minutes.

3. Stir in kidney beans. Cook for about 10 minutes.

4. Using a food processor, purée about half the mixture and return to the saucepan. Return to boil and gradually stir in pasta; continue cooking, stirring often so mixture does not stick to bottom, until pasta is tender. Season with salt and pepper to taste.

5. Serve in large shallow soup bowls and sprinkle with Parmesan cheese.

Serves 8

Nippy Cheese Dreams

1/2 cup	butter, at room temperature	125 mL
1 cup	grated old Cheddar cheese	250 mL
1/2 tsp	Worcestershire sauce	2 mL
1/2 tsp	Tabasco sauce	2 mL
1 cup	all-purpose flour	250 mL

1. Preheat oven to 350° F (180° C).

2. In a bowl, cream together butter, cheese, Worcestershire and Tabasco. Beat in flour.

3. Form dough into two rolls about 1-1/2 inches (3.75 cm) thick. Wrap and chill in refrigerator for 1 hour. Cut into slices 1/4 inch (5 mm) thick.

4. Place slices on baking sheet and bake for 12 to 15 minutes or until golden. Serve hot or cold.

Makes 24 pieces

OLIVE CHEESE BALLS
Make the dough for Nippy Cheese Dreams. Wrap a spoonful of unbaked dough around a pimento-stuffed green olive. Place the olive balls on a baking sheet and bake at 350° F (180° C) for 15 minutes.

Cheese and Cauliflower Soup

This is a great soup for kids. Serve it with some grainy bread for a complete meal.

Cheese is high in protein and, if sealed in moisture-proof wrapping, will keep fresh in the refrigerator for weeks.

A teaspoon of basil, thyme, chives or tarragon will perk up the flavour of any cream soup.

2 tbsp	vegetable oil or butter	25 mL
1	onion, diced	1
3	potatoes, peeled and diced	4
1	head cauliflower, coarsely chopped	1
4 cups	chicken or vegetable stock	1 L
2 cups	milk or light cream	500 mL
2-1/2 cups	grated Cheddar cheese	625 mL

1. In a saucepan, heat oil on medium heat and sauté onions for 2 minutes. Add potatoes and cook, stirring often, for 4 minutes.

2. Add cauliflower and cook for a few minutes more, stirring often. Stir in stock. Cover and cook until cauliflower is tender, about 20 minutes.

3. Purée mixture in blender or food processor. Return to saucepan and add milk and cheese. Cook over low heat for 5 minutes, or until cheese is melted.

Serves 8

Broccoli Tofu Soup

If you don't think you could eat anything as healthy as tofu, try this recipe. Even the kids like it.

8 oz	tofu	250 g
1/4 cup	chopped onion	50 mL
1 cup	chicken stock	250 mL
1/4 tsp	dried basil	1 mL
2 cups	chopped broccoli	500 mL
2	potatoes, peeled and chopped	2
2 cups	milk	500 mL
3/4 cup	grated Swiss cheese	175 mL

1. Place tofu between doubled paper towels. Press gently to extract as much moisture as possible. Cut tofu into 1/2-inch (1.25 cm) cubes.

2. In a saucepan, combine onion, stock and basil. Bring to a boil and stir in broccoli and potatoes. Reduce heat, cover and simmer for 10 minutes, or until potatoes are tender.

3. Gradually add milk. Add cheese and tofu. Stir until cheese is melted.

Serves 4

Tofu, or bean curd, is a staple in the oriental diet, as it contains high-quality protein and is cholesterol-free, low in sodium, and is a good source of calcium. It is made from curdled soy bean milk, and can be purchased in blocks in the vegetable section of the supermarket. Store tofu in the refrigerator, and keep it covered with water.

Broccoli is an excellent source of vitamins A and C, and of fibre.

Pizza Soup

A meal-in-one-bowl dinner. Serve it with garlic bread.
Additional vegetables can be added, such as diced
carrot, celery, sliced zucchini and snow peas.

For chilly winter school days warm this soup and put into a wide-mouth unbreakable thermos for a nutritional packed lunch.

2 tbsp	olive oil	25 mL
2	cloves garlic, finely chopped	2
2	onions, diced	2
1	green pepper, coarsely chopped	1
8 oz	pepperoni, diced	250 g
8 oz	mushrooms, sliced	250 g
1	28-oz (796 mL) can tomatoes, undrained, chopped	1
1	28-oz (796 mL) can tomato sauce	1
1	10-oz (300 g) can beef stock, plus two cans of water	1
2	bay leaves	2
1 tsp	dried basil	5 mL
1 tsp	dried oregano	5 mL
1 cup	macaroni	250 mL
	Coarsely ground pepper to taste	
1 cup	grated mozzarella cheese	250 mL

1. In a large saucepan, heat the olive oil on medium heat. Sauté the garlic, onions and green pepper for 5 minutes.

2. Add the pepperoni and mushrooms and continue to cook for 5 minutes.

3. Add the tomatoes with their juice, tomato sauce, beef stock and water. Add the herbs and the pasta and bring to a boil. Simmer until the pasta is cooked, then season with pepper. Top each serving with grated mozzarella.

Serves 8 to 10

Pacific Chowder

A great fish soup/stew from the West Coast.

1 lb	cod or halibut fillets	500 g
1 tbsp	vegetable oil	15 mL
1/2	small onion, chopped	1/2
2	carrots, thinly sliced	2
2	stalks celery, thinly sliced	2
1	19-oz (540 mL) can tomatoes, drained	1
3/4 cup	cooked shell noodles or macaroni	175 mL
2 cups	water	500 mL
2 tbsp	chopped parsley	25 mL
	Salt and pepper to taste	
	Grated Parmesan cheese (optional)	

The word "chowder" comes from the French *chaudière* – the pot that French fishermen traditionally used for cooking their fish. Chowders are generally thick mixtures of fish, potatoes and other vegetables.

1. Cut fish fillets into bite-sized pieces.

2. In a saucepan, heat oil. Sauté onion, carrots and celery until tender-crisp, about 4 to 5 minutes.

3. Add tomatoes, noodles, water and 1 tbsp (15 mL) parsley. Cover and simmer for 5 minutes.

4. Add fish and cook for 5 minutes. Season to taste with salt and pepper. Serve garnished with the remaining chopped parsley and Parmesan cheese.

Serves 4

Anne Lindsay's Fish Chowder

This is from Anne Lindsay's cookbook Smart Cooking, *published in cooperation with the Canadian Cancer Society (Macmillan). Use any fresh or frozen fillets.*

2 tbsp	butter	25 mL
1	onion, finely chopped	1
3	potatoes, diced	3
1	carrot, finely chopped	1
2 cups	water	500 mL
2 cups	milk	500 mL
1 lb	monkfish or other fresh or frozen fish fillets	500 g
1 cup	kernel corn	250 mL
pinch	salt	pinch
pinch	pepper	pinch
	Chopped parsley to taste	

1. In a heavy saucepan, melt butter on medium heat. Add onion, potatoes and carrot and cook, stirring occasionally, for 5 minutes.

2. Add water; cover and simmer until vegetables are nearly tender, about 10 minutes.

3. Stir in milk, fish (if using monkfish, cut into chunks) and corn. Simmer for 5 to 10 minutes, or until fish flakes and is opaque. Add salt, pepper and parsley.

Serves 4 to 5

2
Chicken
& Seafood

Honey-Glazed Chicken

This is simple to make and delicious.
Serve with cooked rice, noodles and/or dumplings.

8	whole chicken legs	8
1 tsp	salt	5 mL
1/2 tsp	dried basil	2 mL
1/4 tsp	pepper	1 mL
1/2 cup	soy sauce	125 mL
1/2 cup	ketchup	125 mL
1/4 cup	honey	50 mL
1/4 cup	vegetable oil	50 mL
2	large cloves garlic, minced	2

The taste of honey depends on the kinds of flowers from which bees gather the nectar. Clover honey is the most common. If honey has crystallized, it can be heated in the microwave or by placing the jar in a container of hot water. If you don't have honey, corn syrup is a good substitute; use the same amount as you would honey.

1. Preheat oven to 350° F (180° C).

2. Separate chicken legs and thighs and sprinkle with salt, basil and pepper.

3. In a bowl, mix together soy sauce, ketchup, honey, oil and garlic.

4. In a shallow pan, place chicken in a single layer, skin side up, and baste with sauce.

5. Bake, uncovered, for 45 minutes, or until cooked through, basting frequently.

Serves 8

Myra Sable's Chicken Diable

This easy dish comes from The Sable and Rosenfeld Elegant Entertaining Cookbook *(Bantam). Serve it with rice, chutneys and a cucumber and yogurt salad.*

2 lb	chicken legs or breasts	1 kg
1/4 cup	butter	50 mL
1/2 cup	honey	125 mL
1/4 cup	Dijon mustard	50 mL
1 tbsp	curry powder	15 mL
1 tsp	salt	5 mL

1. Preheat oven to 350° F (180° C).

2. In a shallow baking dish, arrange chicken pieces in one layer.

3. In a small saucepan, melt butter. Stir in honey, mustard, curry powder and salt. Pour honey mixture over chicken, turning pieces so they are coated.

4. Cover and bake for 45 minutes. Uncover and bake, basting frequently with sauce, for 15 minutes longer, until chicken is tender and golden.

Serves 4

No-Fuss
Baked Chicken

This is a kid-pleasing recipe — no bones about it!!
Plain yogurt can be substituted for the mayonnaise.

1/4 cup	mayonnaise	50 mL
1 tbsp	prepared mustard	15 mL
2 tbsp	grated Parmesan cheese	25 mL
4	boneless, skinless single chicken breasts	1
2/3 cup	crushed cornflakes	150 mL

1. Preheat oven to 400° F (200° C).

2. In a bowl, combine mayonnaise, mustard and cheese.

3. Brush both sides of chicken with mixture. Coat well with crushed cornflakes.

4. Bake on a greased baking sheet for 25 minutes, or until golden brown and tender.

Serves 4

Mayonnaise is high in fat and cholesterol; substitute low-fat yogurt or use half yogurt and half sour cream.

Creole Chicken

1/4 cup	butter, at room temperature	50 mL
2	cloves garlic, minced	2
2 tbsp	Worcestershire sauce	25 mL
1/2 tsp	Tabasco sauce	2 mL
1 tsp	dried thyme	5 mL
1/2 tsp	dried sage	2 mL
1/2 tsp	pepper	2 mL
1/2 tsp	cayenne pepper	2 mL
4	single chicken breasts	4

Cayenne pepper is hot and adds heat to the taste of your food. Use in moderation unless you enjoy spicy food.

1. Preheat oven to 375° F (190° C).

2. In a bowl, combine butter, garlic, Worcestershire, Tabasco and seasonings and set aside.

3. Place chicken pieces skin side up on a foil-lined baking sheet.

4. Dab chicken with butter mixture and bake for 45 minutes or until the juices run clear, basting occasionally with pan drippings.

Serves 4

Cajun Chicken Fingers

*This dish, from the Canadian Living Test Kitchen, takes
15 minutes to cook, and the children can make it.*

4	boneless, skinless single chicken breasts (about 1 lb/500 g)	4
2 tsp	lemon juice	10 mL
1/3 cup	mayonnaise	75 mL
1/2 tsp	Worcestershire sauce	2 mL
1/4 tsp	dry mustard	1 mL
1	clove garlic, minced	1
1/2 cup	dry breadcrumbs	125 mL
1/4 cup	cornmeal	50 mL
1 tsp	paprika	5 mL
1/2 tsp	dried oregano	2 mL
pinch	cayenne pepper	pinch
1/2 tsp	pepper	2 mL

MICROWAVE METHOD
Arrange half of the chicken fingers evenly on a microwave rack. Microwave, uncovered, at High (100%) for 2 to 3 minutes, or until the chicken is no longer pink inside. Rotate the dish once during cooking. Transfer to a serving dish and cook the second batch.

1. Preheat oven to 425° F (220° C).

2. Cut chicken breasts on diagonal into 1/2-inch (1.25 cm) strips. Set aside.

3. In small bowl, combine lemon juice, mayonnaise, Worcestershire, mustard and garlic; set aside.

4. In a shallow dish, combine breadcrumbs, cornmeal, paprika, oregano, cayenne and pepper, mixing well.

5. Dip chicken into mayonnaise mixture, then into crumb mixture, pressing to coat.

6. Arrange chicken on baking sheet and bake for 15 minutes.

Serves 4

Chinese Chicken Wings

12	whole chicken wings	12
	Pepper to season chicken	
2 tbsp	honey	25 mL
1 tbsp	soy sauce	15 mL
1 tbsp	orange juice	15 mL
1 tbsp	hoisin sauce	15 mL
1/4 tsp	Tabasco sauce (optional)	1 mL

Hoisin sauce is a thick, dark, red-brown condiment made with soy beans, sugar, garlic and vinegar. If you buy it in a can, transfer it to a glass jar with a lid and refrigerate; it should keep indefinitely. In a pinch, mango chutney can be substituted.

1. Cut off wing tips and discard. Cut wings in half, at the joint. Season with pepper.

2. In a large bowl, combine the remaining ingredients. Add chicken and marinate for 30 minutes.

3. Preheat oven to 400° F (190° C).

4. Arrange the wings in a single layer in a baking dish lined with foil. Bake for 35 to 45 minutes, until well browned. Turn the wings twice while baking, and brush them with the remaining marinade.

Serves 4

Honey-Garlic Chicken Wings

Great for sitting in the garden or by the poolside for a light summertime meal.

2 lb	chicken wings	1 kg
2 tbsp	honey	25 mL
1 tbsp	lemon juice	15 mL
1/3 cup	soy sauce	75 mL
1 tsp	ground ginger	5 mL
1	clove garlic, minced	1
1 tbsp	chopped green onion	15 mL

1. Wash chicken wings, cut in half at the joint and discard tips.

2. In large bowl, combine remaining ingredients and mix well. Add wings and marinate in refrigerator for 2 hours.

3. Preheat oven to 350° F (180° C).

4. Arrange wings in a single layer on a foil-lined baking sheet. Bake, uncovered, for 40 minutes, or until juices run clear. Turn wings occasionally during cooking.

Serves 4

Baked Potatoes: When baking potatoes in the oven, insert skewers through the middle to decrease the cooking time–saving power and ensuring the centre is cooked.

Chicken and Rice

Use Italian Arborio rice in this recipe if you can; long-grain rice will give you a dry rather than creamy base for the chicken. Do not use instant rice, which would become overcooked and pasty by the time the chicken is cooked.

Chunks of cooked roast pork, artichoke hearts, fresh firm-fleshed fish (cod, grouper or tilefish), or shelled shrimp, clams or mussels can be added to this dish with the peas.

Long-grain rice should cook to a slightly firm consistency, with separate grains. Short-grain rice absorbs more water than long-grain rice, and should always be used in puddings, or when a creamy consistency is desired. The best short-grain rice is Italian Arborio.

6	whole chicken legs, cut in half	6
	Paprika, salt and pepper to season chicken	
3 tbsp	olive oil	45 mL
2	onions, chopped	2
2	cloves garlic, finely chopped	2
1	small green pepper, cut into 1/2-inch (1.25 cm) pieces	1
1	small red pepper, cut into 1/2-inch (1.25 cm) pieces	1
2	tomatoes, cut into 1/2-inch (1.25 cm) chunks	2
1/2 tsp	turmeric	2 mL
1/2 tsp	paprika	2 mL
1/2 tsp	dried thyme	2 mL
1-1/2 cups	short-grain Italian rice	375 mL
4 cups	chicken stock	1 L
2	bay leaves	2
1 cup	frozen peas	250 mL

1. Preheat oven to 325° F (160° C).

2. Season chicken pieces with salt, pepper and paprika.

3. In a large ovenproof skillet or Dutch oven, heat olive oil on medium-high heat. Sprinkle on chicken seasonings. Sauté chicken slowly for about 15 minutes, turning frequently to brown evenly. Remove chicken and set aside.

4. Sauté onions, garlic and red and green peppers in the oil for 3 minutes.

5. Add tomatoes, turmeric, paprika, thyme and rice and cook, stirring constantly, for 3 minutes.

6. Add chicken stock and bay leaves and slowly bring to a boil, stirring well and scraping up anything sticking to the bottom of the pan. Cover and simmer for about 10 minutes.

7. Add frozen peas, distributing them evenly throughout the dish. Check and adjust seasoning. Add the chicken pieces and bury them in the rice.

8. Cover and bake in oven for 20 minutes. Bake, uncovered, for an additional 10 minutes (the rice should be sticky but not wet).

Serves 6

Chicken Enchiladas

The cooked dish freezes well and should be reheated from the frozen state at 350° F (180° C) for about 40 minutes, or until the sauce is bubbling.

A low-calorie Mexican treat that kids enjoy. Each serving contains approximately 230 calories.

1 tbsp	vegetable oil	15 mL
3	onions, finely chopped	3
2	cloves garlic, finely chopped	2
1 tsp	salt	5 mL
2 tbsp	chili powder	25 mL
1 tsp	ground cumin	5 mL
1	28-oz (796 mL) can tomatoes, undrained	1
2 cups	diced cooked chicken	500 mL
1 cup	grated old Cheddar cheese	250 mL
8	small corn tortillas, warm	8
1 cup	grated mozzarella cheese	250 mL

1. In a large skillet, heat oil over low heat. Stir in onions and garlic and cook, covered, until soft, stirring frequently to prevent scorching.

2. Add salt, chili powder and cumin and mix well. Pour juice from tomatoes into the pan and then chop the tomatoes and add them to the mixture. Continue to cook, covered, for 10 minutes.

3. Pour half of sauce into a large bowl.

4. Add chicken and half the grated Cheddar cheese to the remaining sauce in the skillet and mix well.

5. Preheat oven to 350° F (180° C).

6. Spoon the chicken mixture into the centre of each tortilla and roll the tortilla around it. Place the enchiladas, folded side down, in a greased baking dish large enough to hold the enchiladas in one layer. Spoon the remaining sauce evenly over the tops of the enchiladas and then sprinkle on the remaining Cheddar and mozzarella.

7. Bake, covered, for 30 minutes.

Serves 8

Summertime Chicken Salad

This interesting salad is a hit at buffets. Or you can serve it on individual plates lined with lettuce leaves.

You can use canned pineapple and mandarin oranges in this recipe. In this case, omit the additional juice and use juice reserved from the tins.

1/2 cup	plain yogurt	125 mL
1/2 cup	pineapple juice	125 mL
1/2 cup	orange juice	125 mL
1/2 tsp	ground ginger	2 mL
1/2 tsp	dry mustard	2 mL
3 cups	diced cooked chicken	750 mL
1	fresh pineapple, cut into chunks	1
4	fresh seedless tangerines or oranges, peeled and sectioned	1
2 cups	snow peas	500 mL
3/4 cup	sliced celery	175 mL
1/4 cup	finely chopped green onions	50 mL
2	bananas	2

1. In a small bowl, blend together yogurt, fruit juices, ginger and mustard. Chill in refrigerator.

2. In a large bowl, toss the chicken, pineapple, oranges, snow peas, celery and onions. (Refrigerate at this point if desired.) Just before serving, slice bananas and toss into salad with dressing.

Serves 6 to 8

Moroccan Chicken Salad Sandwiches

Cumin is an ancient spice that has been used since Biblical times. It has a nutty smell and taste and is often used in Mexican and Indian cooking. It comes in powdered and seed form.

2 cups	diced cooked chicken	500 g
1	tomato, diced	1
1	red pepper, diced	1
1/2	cucumber, peeled and diced	1/2
1/4 cup	toasted pine nuts	50 mL
1/2 cup	plain yogurt	125 mL
3 tbsp	mayonnaise	45 mL
3 tbsp	chopped parsley	45 mL
1/2 tsp	ground cumin	2 mL
4	pita breads	4
	Shredded lettuce	

1. In a large bowl, combine chicken, tomato, red pepper, cucumber and nuts. Toss well.

2. In a small bowl, combine yogurt, mayonnaise, parsley and cumin; blend into chicken mixture.

3. To assemble sandwiches, spoon filling into pitas and top with lettuce.

Makes 4 large sandwiches

Lucy Waverman's Sautéed Chicken Livers

Chicken livers are a healthy, inexpensive food that have a bad reputation in some quarters due to poor preparation. Badly cooked, they become dried-up little pebbles on the plate. Well executed, they are exquisite and succulent. For the best flavour and texture, cook them just until they are slightly pink in the middle. This recipe is from Lucy Waverman's Cooking School Cookbook *(Collins).*

1 lb	chicken livers	500 g
1/4 cup	butter	50 mL
1	small onion, chopped	1
1	clove garlic, finely chopped	1
1 tsp	dried rosemary	5 mL
1/4 cup	rice vinegar	50 mL
1/3 cup	orange juice	75 mL

1. Cut chicken livers in half. Remove any fat or sinews.

2. On medium-high heat, melt 2 tbsp (25 mL) butter in a large skillet. Sauté onion and garlic until softened, about 2 minutes.

3. Add rosemary and chicken livers and sauté until browned, about 2 minutes.

4. Add vinegar and orange juice, scrape up any bits on the bottom of the pan and reduce until 1/4 cup (50 mL) liquid remains. Remove from heat and stir in remaining butter. Serve at once.

Serves 4

Sautéed Spanish Shrimp

A quick appetizer for four people, or a main course for two.
Serve it on a bed of rice.

Shrimp is almost always sold frozen. What looks like fresh shrimp is usually defrosted shrimp. It is often sold deveined for aesthetic reasons, but you can eat the vein. When cooked, shrimp turn pink and curl slightly. Do not overcook shrimp, as they quickly become tough and dry.

12 oz	large raw shrimp, shelled and deveined	375 g
1/3 cup	butter	75 mL
1 tbsp	minced green onion	15 mL
4	cloves garlic, minced	4
2 tsp	lemon juice	10 mL
1 tsp	salt	5 mL
2 tbsp	chopped parsley	25 mL
1/4 tsp	grated lemon rind	1 mL
dash	Tabasco sauce	dash

1. Pat shrimp dry with paper towels; set aside.

2. In a large skillet, melt butter over medium heat. Stir in green onion, garlic, lemon juice and salt. Cook until bubbly.

3. Add shrimp and cook, stirring occasionally, for 4 to 5 minutes, or until shrimp turn pink. Stir in parsley, lemon rind and Tabasco. Serve at once.

Serves 2

Fish Fillets with Onions and Peppers

1/4 cup	all-purpose flour	50 mL
1/2 tsp	salt	2 mL
1/4 tsp	pepper	1 mL
1 tsp	paprika	5 mL
1 lb	sole or halibut fillets, cut into serving pieces	500 g
2 tbsp	butter	25 mL
1 tsp	vegetable oil	5 mL
2	onions, sliced	2
1	green pepper, cut into rings	1
1	red pepper, cut into rings	1
1 tbsp	lemon juice	15 mL
1 tbsp	dry white wine or water	15 mL

1. On waxed paper, combine flour, salt, pepper and paprika. Dip pieces of fish in mixture to coat both sides.

2. In a large skillet, heat butter and oil on medium heat. Sauté onions and pepper rings for 5 minutes, or until soft, stirring occasionally.

3. Remove vegetables and keep warm. Add fish to the same pan and brown well on both sides. Return vegetables to pan.

4. Sprinkle with lemon juice and wine. Cover pan and steam gently over low heat for 5 or 6 minutes, or until white juices rise to the top.

Serves 3 to 4

Do not put frozen fish on the counter to defrost. It is important to keep the fish cold so the outside doesn't deteriorate while the inside is still frozen. Defrost frozen fish in the refrigerator.

Salmon Crunch

You can double this recipe and bake it in a 13 x 9 inch (3.5 L) pan.
It also freezes well. Reheat directly from the frozen state at
350° F (180° C) for 45 minutes, or until a metal skewer
inserted in the centre of the casserole comes out hot.

Including the bones in tinned salmon makes it a significant source of dietary calcium.

Fish is an excellent source of protein and is low in fat and calories.

Filling

2	7-1/2-oz (212 mL) cans salmon	2
3	eggs, beaten	3
1 cup	sour cream	250 mL
1/2 cup	grated old Cheddar cheese	125 mL
1/4 cup	mayonnaise	50 mL
1	onion, finely chopped	1
1/4 tsp	Tabasco sauce	1 mL
1/4 tsp	dried dill	1 mL

Crust

1/2 cup	whole wheat flour	125 mL
1 cup	grated old Cheddar cheese	250 mL
1/2 tsp	salt	2 mL
1/2 tsp	paprika	2 mL
1/2 cup	butter, at room temperature	125 mL
1/3 cup	finely chopped or ground almonds	75 mL

1. Preheat oven to 400° F (200° C).

2. In a bowl, combine flaked salmon, including juice and bones (crushed well). Add all other filling ingredients and mix together. Reserve in refrigerator.

3. Mix crust ingredients in food processor or by hand. Reserve 1/4 cup (50 mL) of crust mixture. Press remaining into the bottom of an 8-inch (2 L) square baking dish. Pour filling into the pan and top with reserved crust mixture. Bake for 45 minutes. Serve warm.

Serves 6

Anne Lindsay's Teriyaki Fish Fillets

"Any kind of fish fillets can be used in this recipe, but cod or salmon are the best," says Anne Lindsay, author of The Lighthearted Cookbook *(Key Porter Books). If you don't have a steamer, cook the fish on a plate placed in a wok filled with 1 inch (2.5 cm) of boiling water. Cover and steam until the fish is tender.*

2 tbsp	sherry	25 mL
2 tbsp	water	25 mL
1 tbsp	soy sauce	15 mL
1 tbsp	vegetable oil	15 mL
2 tsp	grated ginger root	10 mL
1 tsp	granulated sugar	5 mL
1	clove garlic, minced	1
1 lb	cod or salmon fillets, (about 3/4 inch/2 cm thick)	500 g

MICROWAVE METHOD
Place the fish and marinade in a microwavable dish. Cover with vented plastic wrap and microwave at High (100%) for 5 minutes, or until the fish is opaque and flakes when tested with a fork.

1. In a large shallow dish, combine sherry, water, soy sauce, oil, ginger, sugar and garlic; stir to mix. Add fish fillets, cover with marinade and arrange in a single layer. Marinate for 20 minutes at room temperature or refrigerate for up to 4 hours, turning once or twice.

2. Remove fillets from marinade and place in single layer in steamer; cover and steam for 5 to 8 minutes, or until fish is opaque and flakes easily when tested with a fork.

3. Meanwhile, place marinade in a small saucepan and heat. Drizzle a little over fish before serving.

Serves 4

Halibut with Garlic and Lemon

This is a simple recipe that is good barbecued or broiled. Serve with steamed rice, Greek olives and a green salad.

Turmeric is the cleaned, boiled, sun-dried and ground root of an East Indian plant. It is an aromatic spice with a nutty taste and turns food a bright-yellow colour. It is such an important spice of the Hindus that it is used in religious rituals.

2 lb	fresh halibut fillets	1 kg
1/2 cup	lemon juice	125 mL
1/2 cup	olive oil	125 mL
10	cloves garlic, minced	10
1 tbsp	chopped parsley	15 mL
1 tsp	cayenne pepper	5 mL
1/4 tsp	turmeric (optional)	1 mL

1. Arrange fish in a shallow dish. Combine the rest of the ingredients and pour over the fish. Cover tightly with plastic wrap and marinate for 2 hours in the refrigerator. Turn fish several times during this time.

2. Remove fish from marinade and place on a baking sheet. Broil until brown, about 3 to 5 minutes on each side. Do not overcook.

Serves 4

Blackened Black Snapper

Any red or black snapper can be used in this dish.
Garlic powder is used in Cajun cooking in blackened dishes,
because it doesn't burn the way fresh garlic would.

1-1/2 lb	snapper fillets	750 g
1/2 tsp	paprika	2 mL
1/2 tsp	cayenne pepper	2 mL
1/2 tsp	hot red chili flakes	2 mL
2 tsp	dried oregano	10 mL
1/2 tsp	pepper	2 mL
1 tsp	garlic powder	5 mL
1/4 cup	milk	50 mL
2 tbsp	vegetable oil	25 mL
2 tbsp	butter	25 mL
1	lemon, cut into wedges	1

Blackening is a Cajun cooking technique in which food is coated with spices and fried at a very high temperature in a cast-iron skillet. The spices darken in colour but should not burn. The blackening seals in the juices of the meat or fish.

1. Rinse fillets and pat dry.

2. In a small bowl, combine paprika, cayenne, chili flakes, oregano, pepper and garlic powder.

3. Brush fillets with milk. Sprinkle spice mixture on each side and press onto surface.

4. Heat oil and butter in a cast-iron skillet until smoking. Sauté snapper on medium-high heat until well blackened, about 4 minutes per side. Squeeze with fresh lemon juice and serve garnished with an extra wedge.

Serves 6

Marion Kane's Seafood Stew

For a soupier version, increase the amounts of tomatoes, wine and fish stock. For an elegant variation, add mussels in their shells. If fresh tomatoes are not available, use 1-1/2 cups (375 mL) of undrained canned Italian plum tomatoes.

1 tbsp	butter	15 mL
1 tbsp	olive or vegetable oil	15 mL
1	small onion, chopped	1
2	cloves garlic, finely chopped	2
6	plum tomatoes, peeled, seeded and cut into chunks	6
1-1/2 cups	white wine	375 mL
2 cups	fish stock	500 mL
1/2 tsp	dried thyme	2 mL
1/2 tsp	dried oregano	2 mL
1/2 tsp	dried basil	2 mL
	Salt and pepper to taste	
8 oz	fresh salmon, skin and bones removed, cut into chunks	250 g
8 oz	fresh monkfish, skin and bones removed, cut into chunks	250 g
8 oz	fresh cod or grouper, skin and bones removed, cut into chunks	250 g
8 oz	fresh scallops	250 g
8 oz	large raw shrimp, peeled and deveined	250 g
2 cups	croutons	500 mL
	Sour cream or plain yogurt	
	Fresh dill	

1. In a large saucepan or Dutch oven, heat butter and oil on medium heat. Add onion and garlic and sauté until softened.

2. Add tomatoes, wine, fish stock and herbs. Bring to boil. Reduce heat to simmer and cook, uncovered, for about 20 minutes, or until slightly reduced. Add salt and pepper. (Stew can be made ahead to this point.)

3. When ready to serve, return broth to boil. Add fish and seafood. Return to boil and cook for about 2 minutes, or just until seafood is opaque. Do not overcook.

4. Ladle stew into large bowls and top each with a handful of croutons, a dollop of sour cream and a sprig of dill.

Serves 6

Pickled Salmon

This recipe keeps for two weeks in the refrigerator. Use as an unusual brunch dish or as a first course.

1-1/2 cups	white vinegar	375 mL
2 cups	water	500 mL
1 tsp	pickling spices	5 mL
1 tsp	salt	5 mL
1	onion, sliced	1
1/2 cup	brown sugar	125 mL
3 lb	salmon steaks	1.5 kg

1. In a large non-aluminum saucepan, combine all the ingredients except the salmon. Bring to a boil and simmer for 20 minutes.

2. Lower heat, add salmon to liquid and simmer for about 10 minutes. Remove salmon to a serving dish and strain liquid. Pour the strained liquid back over the salmon. Chill before serving.

Serves 6 to 8

Atlantic salmon is slightly fattier and more full-bodied in taste and texture than Pacific salmon. It is generally more expensive than the Pacific varieties.

Mono Cliff Mussels

Serve hot or cold with lemon wedges and bread.

Store fresh mussels on ice up to 2 days. Rinse mussels in clean water and pull away beards from the shells. If mussels are open before cooking, discard.

2 tbsp	olive oil	25 mL
2 tsp	cracked black peppercorns	10 mL
24	mussels	24
2 tbsp	diced shallots	25 mL
2 tbsp	finely chopped garlic	25 mL
1/2	diced tomato	1/2
1/4 cup	lemon juice	50 mL
1/4 cup	dry white wine	50 mL
pinch	thyme	pinch
	Salt and freshly ground pepper to taste	
2 tbsp	chopped parsley	75 mL

1. Heat skillet on high heat. Add olive oil and peppercorns and cook until peppercorns start to pop.

2. Carefully add mussels and toss in hot oil until they begin to pop open.

3. Stir in all remaining ingredients and simmer for 1 minute or until flavours are combined.

Serves 2 to 3

Anne Lindsay's
Baked Salmon with Herbs

A delicious recipe from Anne Lindsay's Smart Cooking *(Macmillan) that is great for a weekend family feast or for an elegant dinner party.*

1	whole salmon or piece about 2-1/2 lb (1.2 kg)	1
1/2 cup	chopped fresh parsley	125 mL
2 tbsp	combination of chopped fresh herbs— dill, chives, chervil, basil, sage (optional)	25 mL
	Salt and freshly ground pepper	
1 tbsp	water	15 mL
1 tbsp	lemon juice	15 mL

Plan on about 1/2 lb (250 g) per person for a salmon under 4 lb (166 g); or about 1/3 lb (166 g) per person for a salmon over 4 lb (2 kg) or a chunk piece.

Garnish (optional)

	Cucumber slices, parsley, dill or watercress

1. Place salmon on foil; measure thickness at thickest part. Sprinkle parsley and herbs, and salt and pepper to taste inside cavity.

2. Mix water with lemon juice and sprinkle over outside of salmon. Fold foil over and seal.

3. Place wrapped salmon on baking sheet and bake in 450° F (230° C) oven for 10 minutes for every 1 inch (2.5 cm) thickness of fish, plus an additional 10 minutes' cooking time because it's wrapped in foil (35 to 40 minutes' total cooking time), or until salmon is opaque.

4. Unwrap salmon and discard skin; most of it should stick to foil. Place salmon on warmed platter. Garnish with cucumber, parsley, dill or watercress (if using). Alternatively, arrange cooked vegetables on platter with salmon.

Serves 4

Salmon Puffs

These puffs make an excellent breakfast or brunch dish.
Or serve them with soup and salad for a light dinner.

The various types of canned salmon have about the same nutritional value. The main difference is in the colour and the quality of flesh.

16	soda crackers, well crushed	16
1 cup	milk	250 mL
1	7-1/2-oz (213 g) can salmon, drained	1
2	green onions, finely chopped	2
2	eggs, separated	2
	Salt and pepper to taste	
1 tbsp	melted butter	15 mL
1 tsp	grated Parmesan cheese	5 mL

1. In a large bowl, soak crackers in milk for 30 minutes. Add well-mashed salmon, green onions and egg yolks and combine well. Add salt and pepper.

2. Preheat oven to 325°F (160° C).

3. In separate bowl, beat egg whites until stiff. Fold into salmon mixture.

4. Brush 12 muffin tins with melted butter. Dust with Parmesan cheese. Pour in salmon batter.

5. Bake for 35 to 40 minutes, or until a toothpick inserted comes out clean. Allow to cool slightly before removing from tins.

Makes 12 puffs

3
Beef, Lamb & Pork

Hawaiian Meat Loaf

Some families like this meat loaf even better than roast beef. It's a good idea to make two – one to eat and one to freeze for another occasion – as guests love it, too! Reheat the frozen cooked meat loaf at 350° F (180° C) for 45 minutes, or until hot. Serve with chutney or barbecue sauce on the side.

2 lb	lean ground beef	1 kg
1 lb	sausage meat	500 g
2	eggs, slightly beaten	2
1	14-oz (398 mL) can crushed pineapple, drained	1
1/2 cup	chili sauce	125 mL
1 cup	dry breadcrumbs	250 mL
1 tbsp	horseradish	15 mL
1	clove garlic, minced	1
1 tsp	salt	5 mL
1 tsp	pepper	5 mL

Homemade breadcrumbs: Cut stale bread into even-sized pieces and process in a blender or food processor until fine crumbs appear. Store in the freezer. Try pumpernickel, caraway, sourdough or french bread for different flavours.

1. Preheat oven to 350° F (180° C).

2. In a large bowl, blend all ingredients together. If mixture is too dry, add 1/4 cup (50 mL) pineapple juice.

3. Pat into two greased 9 x 5-inch (2 L) loaf pans.

4. Bake for 1-1/4 hours, or until meat loaf shrinks from pan. Drain off fat. Allow to rest for 5 minutes before cutting.

Each loaf serves 4

Tangy Chuckwagon Pot Roast

This is a great winter make-ahead dish that tastes even better the second day. It is also a great recipe for the slow-cooker. Brown the meat and combine with all other ingredients in the cooker and cook on low for 8 to 9 hours. Heat a loaf of French bread and serve with a salad for an easy meal.

To peel pearl onions, cut the root ends off the onions. Place the onions in a pot of cold water and bring to a boil. Boil for 1 minute and drain. The skins should slide off easily.

3 lb	chuck or blade roast	1.5 kg
1 tsp	salt	5 mL
1/3 cup	all-purpose flour	75 mL
1 tbsp	olive oil	15 mL
1 cup	barbecue sauce	250 mL
1/2 tsp	coarsely ground black pepper	2 mL
1/4 cup	Worcestershire sauce	50 mL
1 tsp	dry mustard	5 mL
1/2 cup	lemon juice	125 mL
1 tbsp	chopped garlic	15 mL
1	10-oz (300 mL) can beef stock, undiluted	1
1-1/2 lb	potatoes, peeled and quartered	750 g
8 oz	carrots, peeled and sliced	250 g
20	pearl onions, blanched and peeled	20

1. Rub roast with salt and flour. In a large ovenproof casserole dish, heat olive oil on medium-high heat and brown roast on all sides. Remove the meat to a platter and pour off any excess fat.

2. Preheat oven to 350° F (180° C).

3. In casserole dish, combine barbecue sauce, pepper, Worcestershire, mustard, lemon juice, garlic and beef stock. Return beef to dish. Cover and roast for 1-1/2 hours.

4. Remove roast from oven, skim off fat and add potatoes, carrots and onions. Cover and gently simmer on stove over medium heat for 1 hour more, or until meat is fork-tender. Remove meat and let sit for 15 minutes before slicing and serving.

Serves 6 to 8

Beef Paprika Goulash

Serve this goulash with wide egg noodles and top it with sour cream.

2 tbsp	vegetable oil	25 mL
2 lb	stewing beef, cubed	1 kg
2	onions, chopped	2
2	cloves garlic, chopped	2
1 tbsp	all-purpose flour	15 mL
2 cups	beef stock	500 mL
1/2 tsp	dried marjoram	2 mL
1/2 tsp	caraway seed	2 mL
1 tsp	brown sugar	5 mL
2 tsp	paprika	10 mL
	Salt and pepper to taste	

Goulash is a Hungarian meat stew or soup. Although this peasant dish varies greatly according to region, caraway seeds are always included, and they give the stew a strong, slightly hot flavour.

1. In a large saucepan, heat oil on high heat. Add beef and cook until brown on all sides. Remove beef from the pan, then add onions and garlic, cooking until transparent. Sprinkle in flour and stir into mixture. Cook for 1 minute.

2. Return beef to pan. Add stock, marjoram, caraway seeds, brown sugar, paprika, salt and pepper. Cover tightly and cook gently for 2 to 2-1/2 hours, or until the meat is tender.

Serves 6

Cheesy Shepherd's Pie

Shepherd's pie is an old Scottish recipe — an easy one-dish meal that was originally made with leftover roast lamb or beef. Shepherds would take this pie to the hillsides and heat it over a wood fire as they watched their flocks.

2 lb	potatoes, peeled and diced	1 kg
3/4 cup	hot milk	175 mL
2 tbsp	butter	25 mL
3/4 cup	grated Cheddar cheese	175 mL
	Salt and pepper to taste	
2 tbsp	vegetable oil	25 mL
2	onions, chopped	
2	cloves garlic, chopped	
2 lb	lean ground beef	1 kg
2 tbsp	all-purpose flour	25 mL
1 cup	milk	250 mL
1	19-oz (540 mL) can tomatoes, drained and chopped	1
1/4 tsp	Tabasco sauce	1 mL
1 tsp	Worcestershire sauce	5 mL
1/2 cup	fresh breadcrumbs	125 mL
1/2 cup	frozen peas	125 mL
1 tsp	paprika	15 mL

1. Place potatoes in a saucepan. Cover with cold water. Bring to a boil and simmer for 20 minutes, or until tender. Drain and mash.

2. In a bowl, combine potatoes with hot milk, butter and cheese. Add salt and pepper to taste. Reserve.

3. In a large saucepan, heat oil. Sauté onions and garlic until softened, about 2 minutes.

4. Add beef and cook until browned. Stir in flour and then milk. Bring to a boil and simmer for 4 minutes.

5. Add tomatoes. Turn heat to low and cook gently until thickened, about 20 minutes.

6. Add Tabasco, Worcestershire, breadcrumbs and peas. Taste for seasoning, adding salt and pepper as needed.

7. Preheat oven to 400° F (200°C).

8. Transfer mixture to a 13 x 9-inch (3.5 L) baking dish. Spread mashed potato mixture on the top and sprinkle with paprika.

9. Bake for 30 minutes, or until potatoes are browned.

Serves 6

Why Meat Needs to Rest Before Slicing

When meat is roasted, the heat forces the natural juices out of the hot tissue towards the centre. If you slice meat right after it comes out of the oven, you will see that the centre is pink but that the outer meat is brown / grey. You will also notice that a lot of juice runs out of the meat and collects in the serving dish. However, if the meat is allowed to cool for at least 10 minutes before carving, the juices that had earlier been forced out by the heat will be reabsorbed by the tissues. This makes the whole roast juicier; it also gives it a uniform colour, so that it will be pink throughout.

Wayne Gretzky's Chili

This is the recipe that makes Wayne score! If you don't want to use red wine, substitute 2 tbsp (25 mL) of red wine vinegar. Serve the chili with lots of different toppings, such as grated cheese, sour cream, chopped onions, or even grated bittersweet chocolate!

2 lb	ground beef	1 kg
2	onions, chopped	2
4	cloves garlic, chopped	4
1	5-1/2-oz (156 mL) can tomato paste	1
1	28-oz (796 mL) can tomatoes, undrained	1
1	19-oz (540 mL) can crushed pineapple, drained	1
1/2 cup	red wine	125 mL
2 tbsp	chili powder	25 mL
1 tsp	Tabasco sauce	5 mL
1 tsp	Worcestershire sauce	5 mL
1	green pepper, chopped	1
1 tsp	salt	5 mL
1/2 tsp	pepper	2 mL
1	19-oz (540 mL) can kidney beans, drained	1

1. Combine all the ingredients except beans in a large saucepan and simmer, covered, for 1-1/2 hours, or until tender. Add beans and simmer for 10 minutes.

Serves 8

Beef with Onions

1-1/2 lb	chuck steak	750 g
2 tbsp	butter	25 mL
1 tbsp	vegetable oil	15 mL
1	onion, sliced	1
1 tbsp	all-purpose flour	15 mL
1-1/2 cups	beef stock	375 mL
1	clove garlic, minced	1
1/2 tsp	ground cumin	2 mL
pinch	dried marjoram	pinch
2 tbsp	red wine vinegar	25 mL
	Salt and pepper to taste	

There are lots of varieties of onions. Cooking onions are the most common; they are full-flavoured but not very sweet. Because of their sharp flavour, they shouldn't be used raw. Spanish onions and red onions are mild and can be eaten raw. Red onions look especially attractive in salads, though they will lose some of their colour when cooked.

1. Cut meat across the grain into thin finger-length strips.

2. In a large skillet, heat butter and oil on low heat. Add onions and cook, covered, until transparent. Turn them frequently so that they cook evenly but do not brown. Remove from pan.

3. Increase heat, put strips of meat into pan and brown them. Return onions. Sprinkle with flour and stir. When flour begins to colour, stir in stock, garlic, cumin, marjoram, vinegar, salt and pepper. Cover and simmer for 1 hour.

Serves 4

David Wood's Braised Beef Ribs with Olives

Sun-dried tomatoes are sweet and summery. They can be bought either dried or stored in oil. The tomatoes in oil tend to be a little softer.

David Wood feels that ribs are one of those cuts that blossom with long, slow cooking; they develop a tender, still slightly chewy texture and absorb the flavours of all the seasonings. The perfect accompaniment to this dish is a green salad and polenta. This casserole can be made up to two days in advance. Refrigerate and reheat the cold casserole for 1 hour instead of 30 minutes after adding the olives.

3 tbsp	olive oil	45 mL
4 lb	beef short ribs	2 kg
2	onions, sliced	2
1/2 tsp	dried thyme	2 mL
2	bay leaves	2
1/2 tsp	dried rosemary	2 mL
1	strip orange rind	1
	Salt and pepper to taste	
1	14-oz (398 mL) can plum tomatoes, drained and chopped	1
1 cup	strong beef or veal stock	250 mL
3/4 cup	black olives, pitted and chopped	175 mL
1/4 cup	sun-dried tomatoes, chopped	50 mL
3 tbsp	chopped Italian parsley	45 mL

1. Preheat oven to 325 F (160 C).

2. In an ovenproof casserole dish, heat the oil on high heat. Brown the ribs. Remove ribs and set aside.

3. In the same dish, sauté the onions in the fat and oil. Turn the heat down, cover and cook the onions until soft and golden, stirring occasionally – about 20 minutes.

4. Stir in the thyme, bay leaves, rosemary and orange rind. Season with salt and pepper and add the tomatoes. Place the browned ribs on top, pour in stock and bring to a boil.

5. Cover and bake in oven for 2 hours. Check two or three times to ensure there is plenty of liquid; dish should be cooking at a gentle simmer. Turn down heat and add more liquid if necessary.

6. Stir in the olives and sun-dried tomatoes. Return the casserole to the oven for 30 minutes or until completely hot.

7. Sprinkle the ribs with chopped Italian parsley and serve on warm plates.

Serves 4

Temperature Conversions

200° F =	95° C		375° F =	190° C
225° F =	110° C		400° F =	200° C
250° F =	120° C		425° F =	220° C
275° F =	135° C		450° F =	230° C
300° F =	150° C		475° F =	250° C
325° F =	160° C		500° F =	260° C
350° F =	175° C			

Tenderloin of Beef Casserole

Juniper berries have a strong flavour, and are often used in cabbage or game dishes. You can steep a few berries in vodka overnight to give it a gin flavour. To crush the juniper berries, place them in a plastic bag and crush them with a rolling pin.

2 lb	beef filet	1 kg
1 tsp	crushed juniper berries or gin	5 mL
1 tsp	dried thyme	5 mL
1 tsp	pepper	5 mL
2	onions, sliced	2
1 cup	red wine	250 mL
1/4 cup	butter	50 mL
1	clove garlic, minced	1
2 tbsp	chopped parsley	25 mL
1	anchovy, chopped	1
	Salt and pepper to taste	

1. Preheat oven to 425° F (220° C).

2. Trim tail from filet. Slice filet into six equal portions. Place in ovenproof casserole and sprinkle with juniper berries, thyme and pepper. Top with onions. Add wine and dot with butter.

3. Bake for 20 minutes.

4. In a small bowl, combine garlic, parsley, anchovy, salt and pepper and add to the casserole. Bake for another 15 minutes. Serve filet with some sauce spooned over.

Serves 6

Braised Pot Roast

This succulent dish is full of moppable gravy.
It can be served hot or cold.

1/4 cup	all-purpose flour	50 mL
1 tsp	salt	5 mL
1 tsp	pepper	5 mL
1 tsp	paprika	5 mL
1/2 tsp	dried marjoram	2 mL
4 to 5 lb	pot roast (brisket, round, rump, etc.)	2 to 2.5 kg
1/4 cup	vegetable oil	50 mL
1	bay leaf	1
4	onions, cut in half	4
4	carrots, cut in half	4
1/4 tsp	whole cloves	1 mL
1 tbsp	brown sugar	5 mL
1/3 cup	white vinegar	75 mL
1/2 cup	tomato juice or chili sauce	125 mL

A pot roast is a whole chunk of beef — either brisket, round or rump. The meat is browned in a deep pot and then slowly cooked with vegetables and a little liquid until it is fork-tender.

1. In a small bowl, combine flour, salt, pepper, paprika and marjoram. Place on waxed paper.

2. Roll pot roast in mixture until well coated.

3. In a large ovenproof casserole, heat oil on medium heat. Brown meat on all sides for about 20 minutes. Drain excess fat after browning.

4. Preheat oven to 325° F (160° C).

5. Add bay leaf, onions, carrots, cloves, sugar, vinegar and tomato juice to pot roast. Cover and bake for 3 to 4 hours, or until meat is tender.

Serves 10

Ed Mirvish's Cabbage Rolls

Cabbage is an inexpensive and nutritious vegetable. All varieties, from the lacy-leafed Savoy cabbage to the more common red and green, are high in vitamin C and potassium, and low in calories.

2	cabbages	2
1	egg	1
1	onion, grated	1
1	carrot, grated	1
1/3 cup	water	75 mL
	Salt and pepper to taste	
1 lb	medium ground beef	500 g
1/2 cup	uncooked rice	125 mL
2	28-oz (796 mL) cans tomatoes, undrained	2
	Juice of 2 lemons	
1/3 cup	brown sugar	75 mL
1	stalk celery, chopped	1
1	bay leaf	1
1 cup	beef stock	250 mL

1. Preheat oven to 350° F (180° C).

2. Place cabbages in large pot of salted boiling water. Cover and cook for 5 minutes. Drain, run cold water over and drain again. Remove leaves and trim ribs off cabbage leaves for easier rolling. Pat leaves to remove excess moisture.

3. In a large bowl, combine egg, onion, carrot, water, salt and pepper. Add meat and rice and mix thoroughly.

4. Place heaping spoonful of mixture at core end of each cabbage leaf. Roll up mixture, folding sides of leaf in. Fasten with toothpicks. Repeat with remaining leaves.

5. In an 8-cup (2 L) casserole, combine tomatoes, lemon juice, sugar, celery, bay leaf and stock. Add bits of shredded or sliced cabbage to taste.

6. Place cabbage rolls in this sauce and cover tightly. Bake for 30 minutes. Reduce heat to 300° F (150° C) and bake for 1-1/2 hours longer. Check dish occasionally to see that the cabbage rolls have not boiled dry. If necessary, add a small quantity of beef stock.

Serves 6 to 8

Piccadillo

Not to be confused with piccalilli, the relish. This is a wonderful mixture of spiced meat, raisins, olives and tomatoes. Serve it over hot rice or over polenta, or use it as a filling for meat pie.

Compare: Lean ground beef contains not more than 17% fat, medium ground beef 23% fat and regular ground beef 30% fat.

3 tbsp	olive oil	45 mL
1-1/2 lb	lean ground beef	750 g
2	onions, chopped	2
2	large cloves garlic, finely chopped	2
3	tomatoes, peeled and chopped	3
4	canned jalapeño peppers, sliced	4
1/2 cup	raisins	125 mL
1/2 cup	pimento-stuffed olives, sliced	125 mL
1/4 tsp	dried thyme	1 mL
1/4 tsp	dried oregano	1 mL
1 tsp	salt	5 mL

1. Heat oil in a large skillet on medium-high heat. Brown the meat. Add onions and garlic and cook until onions are soft.

2. Stir in remaining ingredients and simmer, uncovered, for about 20 minutes, until raisins have plumped and nearly all the liquid has been absorbed.

Serves 4

Margaret Fraser's Cranberry Pot Roast

Tart berries and the unmistakable flavour of cloves adds a change of pace to an everyday pot roast. This dish can be cooked on the stove top, or at 300° F (150° C) in the oven.

In Canada, cranberries are mainly grown in Ontario and the Maritimes. They are rich in vitamin C and, because of their high acidity, they will keep for several weeks in the refrigerator, and can be frozen for up to six months.

2 tbsp	all-purpose flour	25 mL
1 tsp	salt	5 mL
1/4 tsp	pepper	1 mL
3 lb	chuck, blade or shortrib boneless roast of beef	1.5 kg
3 tbsp	vegetable oil	45 mL
4	whole cloves	4
1/2 cup	beef stock	125 mL
1-1/2 cups	cranberries	375 mL
1/2 cup	brown sugar	125 mL
2 tsp	white vinegar	10 mL
1 tbsp	cornstarch	15 mL

1. In a small bowl, blend together flour, salt and pepper. Rub into roast, covering entire surface.

2. In a Dutch oven, heat oil over medium-high heat. Brown roast on all sides, adding more oil if necessary. Add cloves, stock and cranberries. Reduce heat, cover and simmer for 1-1/2 hours.

3. Add brown sugar and vinegar. Return to boil, reduce heat and simmer for about 30 minutes more, or until meat is fork-tender.

4. Remove meat to heated platter; keep warm. Blend cornstarch with 1 tbsp (15 mL) cold water. Stir into hot cranberry drippings. Cook, stirring, until sauce boils and thickens. Serve over slices of meat.

Serves 6

Chili Beef Burgers

Chili powder and cumin subtly accent this beef burger. Try serving it wrapped in a flour tortilla and topped with sour cream.

1	egg	1
1/4 cup	fresh breadcrumbs	50 mL
1/4 cup	finely chopped green onions	50 mL
2 tbsp	barbecue sauce	25 mL
1/2 tsp	chili powder	2 mL
3/4 tsp	salt	4 mL
1/2 tsp	pepper	2 mL
1/4 tsp	paprika	1 mL
1/4 tsp	ground cumin	1 mL
1/2 tsp	Tabasco	2 mL
1 lb	medium ground beef	500 g

Chili powder is a combination of ground hot chili peppers, cumin, garlic, oregano, cloves and allspice – the mixture was invented in the late nineteenth century in the United States. There is no official recipe; many people make their own.

1. Beat egg in large bowl; mix in breadcrumbs, onions, barbecue sauce, chili powder, salt, pepper, paprika, cumin and Tabasco. Blend in beef; shape mixture into four patties.

2. Place patties on greased grill or broiler rack about 4 inches (10 cm) from medium-high heat. Barbecue for 5 minutes; turn and continue barbecuing for about 5 minutes, or until desired doneness.

Serves 4

Anne Murray's Hearty Hodgepodge

Anne Murray's favourite recipe is great for a crowd, she says.

2 tbsp	olive oil	25 mL
2 lb	ground chuck	1 kg
2	onions, chopped	2
1-1/2 cups	chopped celery	375 mL
3	cloves garlic, chopped	3
2	10-oz (300 mL) cans beef stock, plus 2 cans water	2
1	28-oz (796 mL) can tomatoes, undrained	1
2 tbsp	Worcestershire sauce	25 mL
2 tsp	dried oregano	10 mL
2 tsp	dried basil	10 mL
2	19-oz (540 mL) cans red kidney beans, drained	2
2 cups	elbow macaroni	500 mL

1. In a Dutch oven, heat oil on medium heat. Sauté beef, onions, celery and garlic until beef is browned and onions are tender, about 5 minutes.

2. Stir in beef stock, water, tomatoes, Worcestershire, oregano and basil.

3. Simmer, covered, for 10 minutes. Add kidney beans and macaroni and simmer until macaroni is cooked, about 30 minutes. If mixture thickens too much before pasta is cooked, add a little water.

Serves 8 to 10

Sweet and Tart Shortribs

This dish is best if prepared the day before and allowed to sit overnight in the refrigerator, after which the congealed fat can be skimmed off. Reheat for about 45 minutes before serving. Serve on bed of egg noodles with mashed turnips or carrots.

Shortribs are sold on the bone, and are layered with beef and fat. They are an inexpensive cut, and although they are tough and require long, slow cooking, the final result is tender and juicy.

	Salt and pepper to taste	
3 lb	beef shortribs	1.5 kg
1/2 cup	all-purpose flour	125 mL
4	onions, chopped	4
1/4 cup	olive oil	50 mL
3	large cloves garlic, minced	3
5 cups	crushed canned tomatoes	1.25 L
1 cup	dry vermouth or white wine	250 mL
1 tsp	dried thyme	5 mL
1 tsp	dried rosemary	5 mL
1 tsp	dried oregano	5 mL
3/4 cup	raisins	175 mL
pinch	cinnamon	pinch
1/4 cup	chopped parsley	50 mL

1. Preheat oven to 325° F (160° C).

2. Salt and pepper the ribs. Dredge in flour, reserving excess.

3. Heat olive oil in a heavy skillet on medium-high heat. Brown ribs.

4. Sprinkle on remaining flour and remove the browned ribs. Cook onions in olive oil until translucent.

5. Add the garlic, ribs, crushed tomatoes, vermouth, herbs and raisins.

6. Bake, covered, for 2 hours, or until ribs are tender, stirring occasionally. Sprinkle with pinch of cinnamon and parsley before serving.

Serves 6

Sandie Rinaldo's Chili

This is an easy recipe for those who think they can't cook. Sandie Rinaldo suggests that you soak in a hot bubble bath before preparing this dish, to help you relax and prepare for the ordeal!

1 tbsp	butter	15 mL
1	red onion, chopped	1
1	green pepper, chopped	1
1 lb	lean ground beef	500 g
2	cloves garlic, minced	1
2 tbsp	chili powder	25 mL
1	bay leaf	1
	Salt and pepper to taste	
1	5-1/2 oz (156 mL) can tomato paste	1
1	19-oz (540 mL) can kidney beans, drained	1
1 cup	tomato sauce	250 mL
6	large mushrooms, sliced	6

1. Heat butter in a large saucepan on medium heat. Add onion and green pepper and sauté until tender.

2. Add meat and brown lightly. Season with garlic, chili powder, bay leaf, salt and pepper.

3. Add tomato paste and let mixture simmer, uncovered, on low heat for 10 minutes. Add kidney beans and tomato sauce and bring mixture to a boil. Reduce heat to low and simmer, covered, for 1 hour.

4. Just before serving, add sliced mushrooms and cook for 5 minutes.

Serves 4

Veal with Mushrooms

2 lb	boneless veal cutlets, thinly sliced	1 kg
1/2 cup	all-purpose flour	125 mL
1 tsp	salt	5 mL
1/4 tsp	pepper	1 mL
2 tbsp	vegetable oil	25 mL
3 tbsp	butter	45 mL
1 lb	mushrooms, sliced	500 g
1/3 cup	white wine	75 mL
2 tbsp	lemon juice	25 mL
	Lemon slices for garnish	

The best veal cutlets come from the leg of veal. Although they are quite expensive, pounding them until they are very thin can make the meat go a long way. Thinly sliced and pounded pork cutlets can be substituted if veal is unavailable.

1. Gently pound veal into very thin pieces.

2. In a bowl, mix flour, salt and pepper. Lightly flour veal.

3. In a large skillet, melt oil and butter on medium-high heat. Sauté veal until golden-brown, about 3 minutes per side. Remove and keep warm.

4. Add mushrooms to the saucepan and cook for several minutes. Add wine and lemon juice. Boil rapidly to reduce sauce slightly. Pour over veal and garnish with lemon slices.

Serves 6

Veal Stew

This recipe can be family fare, but it really is delicious enough to be served to friends at a casual dinner party.

To thicken stews, make a *beurre manie.* In a small bowl, combine 2 tbsp (25 mL) butter with 3 tbsp (45 mL) flour until you have a thick paste. Stir this paste into the stew and simmer for a few minutes.

1/3 cup	butter or olive oil	75 mL
1 cup	chopped leeks (white part only)	250 mL
1/2 cup	chopped parsley	125 mL
12 oz	fresh mushrooms, halved	375 g
2-1/2 to 3 lb	veal stewing meat	1.25 to 1.5 kg
1/4 cup	all-purpose flour	50 mL
	Salt and pepper to taste	
2 cups	chicken stock	500 mL
1 cup	sour cream	250 mL
1 tsp	Worcestershire sauce	5 mL
6	large carrots, cut in chunks	6

1. Preheat oven to 325° F (160° C).

2. In a large skillet, melt butter on medium-high heat. Add leeks, parsley and mushrooms. Cook until limp and slightly browned and remove with a slotted spoon to an ovenproof casserole dish.

3. In a bag, toss the veal with the flour, salt and pepper. In the same skillet, cook meat in batches, until brown on all sides. Remove to casserole.

4. In a bowl, combine stock and sour cream until smooth. Add Worcestershire. Pour this mixture over meat and vegetables.

5. Bake for 1 hour. Add carrots and bake for another 45 minutes.

Serves 6

Anne Lindsay's Lamb Loins with Rosemary and Peppercorns

Use lamb loins or tenderloins, usually available in the frozen food section of supermarkets. From Anne Lindsay, author of The Lighthearted Cookbook *(Key Porter Books).*

When using frozen lamb, let the meat defrost in its vacuum pack overnight in the refrigerator. This will prevent the juices from leaking out.

1-1/2 tsp	whole peppercorns, crushed	7 mL
1 tbsp	chopped fresh rosemary leaves, or 1 tsp (5 mL) dried	15 mL
2 tbsp	chopped fresh mint leaves (optional)	25 mL
2	cloves garlic, minced	2
2 tbsp	sherry or red wine vinegar	25 mL
1 tbsp	soy sauce	15 mL
1 lb	lamb tenderloins	500 g

1. In a small bowl, combine peppercorns, rosemary, mint, garlic, sherry and soy sauce. Mix well and pour over lamb. Cover and marinate at room temperature for 30 minutes, or refrigerate for 1 to 6 hours.

2. Remove lamb from marinade. Broil or grill over hot coals for 4 to 6 minutes, or until meat is still pink inside. Turn once or twice during cooking. Cut loins diagonally into thin slices.

Serves 4

Moussaka

This Greek dish of layered meat and eggplant is great for parties. It can be made ahead, and it reheats well. The cinnamon and nutmeg bring out the flavour of the lamb. Serve with a Greek salad.

Eggplant is an oval-shaped vegetable with a shiny purple skin. It should be of uniform colour, firm, smooth and free of any blemishes.

3	medium eggplants	3
1/4 cup	olive oil	50 mL
3	large onions, chopped	3
2 lb	ground lamb	1 kg
3 tbsp	tomato paste	45 mL
1/2 cup	dry red wine	125 mL
1/4 cup	chopped parsley	50 mL
1/4 tsp	cinnamon	1 mL
	Salt and pepper to taste	
1/4 cup	butter	50 mL
1/4 cup	all-purpose flour	50 mL
4 cups	milk	1 L
1/4 tsp	nutmeg	1 mL
4	eggs	4
2 cups	ricotta or cottage cheese	500 mL
1 cup	fine breadcrumbs	250 mL
1 cup	grated Parmesan cheese	250 mL

1. Preheat oven to 350° F (180° C).

2. Peel eggplants and cut into 1/2-inch (1.25 cm) slices. Brush with 2 tbsp (25 mL) oil. Broil eggplant slices for about 3 minutes per side, or until browned. Reserve.

3. In a skillet, heat remaining olive oil on medium heat. Cook onions until soft, about 2 minutes. Add meat and cook until browned, about 10 minutes.

4. In a bowl, mix tomato paste, wine, parsley and cinnamon. Add to the meat. Bring to a boil and then simmer, uncovered, until all liquid is absorbed, about 10 minutes. Season with salt and pepper.

5. In a saucepan, heat the butter. Add the flour and cook for 1 minute. Add the milk and cook, stirring frequently, until thick. Cool a little and add eggs one at a time, beating well. Add the nutmeg, ricotta cheese and salt and pepper to taste. (The sauce will be thick.)

6. Dust a greased 13 x 9-inch (3.5 L) pan with breadcrumbs. Add alternate layers of eggplant and meat. Sprinkle each layer with Parmesan and breadcrumbs. Pour the cheese sauce over top.

7. Bake for 1 hour, or until top is golden. Cool for 30 minutes before serving.

Serves 8 to 10

Common Ingredients
(Approximate Equivalents)

	1 cup =	100 grams =
All-purpose flour	150 grams	2/3 cup
Granulated sugar	210 grams	1/2 cup
Icing sugar	135 grams	3/4 cup
Light brown sugar	200 grams	1/2 cup
Rolled oats	95 grams	1 cup
Graham cracker crumbs	120 grams	4/5 cup
Cocoa powder	125 grams	4/5 cup
Chocolate chips	175 grams	generous 1/2 cup
Sultanas, raisins	165 grams	generous 1/2 cup
Almonds - sliced	75 grams	1-2/3 cups
Almonds - ground	120 grams	4/5 cup
Hazelnuts - whole	140 grams	3/4 cup
Hazelnuts - ground	105 grams	1 cup
Walnut halves	110 grams	1 cup
Walnut pieces	120 grams	4/5 cup
Pecans - whole	110 grams	1 cup
Peanut butter	225 grams	scant 1/2 cup

Bonnie Stern's Marmalade-Glazed Leg of Lamb

Bonnie Stern's recipe from The CKFM Bonnie Stern Cookbook *(Random House) is a favourite at her house.*

1	leg of lamb, butterflied (approx. 4 lb/2 kg after boning)	1
1 tbsp	vegetable oil	15 mL
1/2 cup	marmalade	125 mL
1 tbsp	minced fresh ginger root	15 mL
1	clove garlic, minced	1
1/4 cup	Dijon mustard	50 mL
2 tbsp	soy sauce	25 mL
1 tsp	Worcestershire sauce	5 mL
1/2 tsp	Tabasco sauce	2 mL

1. Pat lamb dry and flatten out as much as possible. Remove any excess fat. Brush lightly with the oil.

2. Preheat the barbecue or broiler.

3. In a small saucepan, combine ingredients for glaze and heat.

4. Cook lamb for 15 minutes per side for rare. Brush with glaze a few times during cooking. Allow lamb to rest for 5 to 10 minutes before carving. Slice thinly.

Serves 6 to 8

Roast Leg of Lamb with Mint Yogurt Hollandaise

A low-calorie but flavourful version of hollandaise accompanies a garlic-studded roast leg of lamb. Try the light hollandaise with salmon or eggs Benedict, too.

1	3-1/2-lb (1.75 kg) short cut leg of lamb, defrosted	1
2	cloves garlic, slivered	2
2 tbsp	butter, at room temperature	25 mL
1 tbsp	Dijon mustard	15 mL
1/2 tsp	dried thyme	2 mL
	Salt and pepper to taste	
3/4 cup	plain yogurt	175 mL
3	egg yolks, beaten slightly	3
3 tbsp	chopped fresh mint	45 mL

Rare lamb will be tough, overcooked lamb will be dry—the best is medium-rare; it will be tender, juicy and pink inside.

Fresh garden mint is easy to freeze and can be frozen in the fall for use during the winter months.

1. Pat lamb dry and make several small, deep incisions with a sharp knife. Insert slivered garlic into incisions.

2. In a small bowl, cream together butter, mustard, thyme, salt and pepper. Rub over outside of lamb. (Recipe can be prepared ahead to this point, covered and refrigerated. Bring out to room temperature 30 minutes before roasting.)

3. Preheat oven to 450° F (230° C).

4. Set lamb flat side down on rack in shallow pan and roast for 10 minutes. Reduce heat to 350° F (180° C) and continue roasting for 1 hour and 15 minutes, or until internal temperature is 130° F (54° C) for rare. Let sit, loosely covered with foil, for 10 minutes before carving.

5. Just before meat is cooked, prepare the hollandaise by stirring together yogurt, egg yolks and salt and pepper to taste in top of double boiler over simmering water. Whisk for 8 to 10 minutes, or until foamy and thickened. Whisk in mint and serve in heated sauceboat.

Serves 6

Wendy Mesley's Roast Leg of Lamb

Wendy Mesley makes this for a special dinner when she and Peter Mansbridge get together on weekends. Serve it with steamed snow peas and baby carrots and roast potatoes. Leftovers are great!

1	4 to 5-lb (2 to 2.5 kg) leg of lamb	1
1/4	lemon	1/4
1	clove garlic, slivered	1
1/2 cup	Dijon mustard	125 mL
2 tsp	dried rosemary	10 mL
1 tsp	dried basil	5 mL

1. Rub lamb all over with lemon. Cut slits in lamb leg and insert garlic slivers. Rub entire roast liberally with mustard. Sprinkle with rosemary and basil. Let stand, covered, for 2 to 3 hours in refrigerator. Place on a rack in shallow roasting pan.

2. Preheat oven to 450° F (230° C).

3. Place uncovered roast in oven. Reduce heat immediately to 350° F (180° C). Roast for 25 to 30 minutes per pound (500 g).

Serves 6

Lamb Chop Satay

*A satay is really a skewer filled with bite-sized pieces of meat,
but this quick and easy version uses tender loin chops.*

8	lamb loin chops, defrosted	8
1/2	small onion, finely chopped	1/2
1	clove garlic, finely chopped	1
2 tbsp	peanut butter	30 mL
1 tbsp	lemon juice	15 mL
1 tbsp	vegetable oil	15 mL
1 tbsp	soy sauce	15 mL
1 tsp	granulated sugar	5 mL
pinch	hot red chili flakes	pinch

Peanut butter is a good source of protein and carbohydrates. Try to avoid buying peanut butter with added hydrogenated oil, sugar, salt or jams and jellies.

1. Dry chops well. Slash each edge once and place chops in shallow glass dish or plastic bag.

2. In a small bowl or food processor, blend together onion, garlic, peanut butter, lemon juice, oil, soy sauce, sugar and chili flakes. Process until fairly smooth. Pour over chops, cover and let sit at room temperature for 30 minutes or refrigerate for up to 8 hours. (Bring out to room temperature for 30 minutes before grilling.)

3. Set chops on greased grill and barbecue 4 inches (10 cm) from medium-hot coals for 4 to 5 minutes per side for rare, turning once.

Serves 4

Jay Nelson's Chili

Absolutely scrumptious, and the chef advises that you allow plenty of preparation time. If possible, have the pork and beef ground together coarsely by the butcher. Serve in hot bowls with a dollop of sour cream and lime wedges, if desired.

1 tbsp	olive oil	15 mL
1 lb	coarsely ground lean pork	500 g
1 lb	coarsely ground lean beef	500 g
2 cups	finely chopped onions	500 mL
1 cup	finely chopped green pepper	250 mL
1 cup	finely chopped celery	250 mL
1 tbsp	minced garlic	15 mL
1 tbsp	dried oregano	15 mL
2	bay leaves	2
2 tsp	ground cumin	10 mL
2 tbsp	chili powder	25 mL
3 cups	tomatoes	750 mL
1	10-oz (300 g) can beef stock, diluted with 1 can water	1
	Salt and pepper to taste	
1/2 tsp	hot red chili flakes	2 mL
2 cups	drained kidney beans	500 mL
	Sour cream and lime wedges as garnish	

1. In a large heavy saucepan, heat oil on medium-high heat. Add meat. Cook, chopping down and stirring with the side of a heavy metal kitchen spoon to break up the lumps.

2. Add onions, green pepper, celery, garlic, oregano, bay leaves, cumin and chili powder. Stir to blend well.

3. Add the tomatoes, stock, water, salt, pepper and chili flakes. Bring to a boil and cook, stirring often, for about 20 minutes. Add the beans and cook for 10 minutes longer.

Serves 8 to 10

Pork should be cooked
until the juices run
clear or a medium
doneness is reached.

Pot Roast Pork with Apples

	Salt and pepper to taste	
2 tsp	cinnamon	10 mL
3 lb	rolled pork roast	1.5 kg
1/4 cup	butter	50 mL
8	Granny Smith apples, peeled and cored	8

1. Preheat oven to 400° F (200° C).

2. In a shallow dish, combine salt, pepper and 1 tsp (5 mL) cinnamon. Roll pork in mixture, covering on all sides.

3. In a large ovenproof casserole, melt 2 tbsp (25 mL) butter on medium heat. Brown pork slowly on all sides. Cover casserole and cook on the middle shelf of the oven for about 1-1/2 hours, turning joint over halfway through roasting time.

4. In a large saucepan, heat the remaining 2 tbsp (25 mL) butter and 1 tsp (5 mL) cinnamon. Add apples, cover and cook for about 10 minutes over low heat, shaking the pan to prevent sticking.

5. Arrange apples around the roast 15 minutes before the end of cooking time. Remove pork from casserole. Slice and place on warmed serving plate. Surround with apples. Serve with pan juices.

Serves 4 to 6

Sticky Spareribs

This recipe can also be used with chicken.

It is always a good idea to parboil spareribs before baking or barbecuing. This will reduce the fat and keep the ribs juicy. If you are baking spareribs, line the baking dish with foil to help with the cleanup.

2 lb	spareribs	1 kg
1/3 cup	honey	75 mL
1/3 cup	soy sauce	75 mL
1 tbsp	white vinegar	15 mL
2 tbsp	sherry	25 mL
2 tbsp	granulated sugar	25 mL
2	cloves garlic, minced	2
2 tsp	ground ginger	10 mL
1 cup	beef stock	250 mL

1. Bring a large saucepan of water to a boil. Cook spareribs for 20 minutes.

2. Preheat oven to 450° F (230° C).

3. In a bowl, mix honey, soy sauce, vinegar, sherry, sugar, garlic, ginger and beef stock.

4. Place spareribs in baking dish and pour honey mixture over. Bake for approximately 20 minutes, until golden-brown and sticky.

Serves 2

Pork Tenderloin and Mushrooms

You only need one hour and one frying pan to make this dish.

1/4 cup	vegetable oil	50 mL
1 lb	pork tenderloin, cut into cubes	500 g
1 cup	beef stock	250 mL
8 oz	mushrooms, sliced	250 g
1	green pepper, diced	1
1	onion, diced	1
2 tbsp	Worcestershire sauce	25 mL
	Salt and pepper to taste	
2 tbsp	red wine	25 mL
1	clove garlic, minced	1
1/2 cup	sour cream	125 mL

Pork tenderloin has little fat and is the leanest cut of pork.

Pork tenderloin has less fat than a prime rib roast.

1. In a skillet, heat oil on medium-high heat. Brown pork on all sides and remove.

2. Add beef stock, mushrooms, green peppers, onion, Worcestershire, salt, pepper, wine and garlic to skillet. Bring to a boil.

3. Return pork to skillet and simmer for 15 minutes, until pork is cooked.

4. Just before serving, stir in sour cream.

Serves 2

Cynthia Wine's
Red-Hot Spareribs

Serve these with cornbread and fresh corn on the cob,
for a complete finger-food meal!

6	cloves garlic, minced	6
2	onions, chopped	2
2-1/4 cups	tomato sauce	550 mL
2	bay leaves	2
1/3 cup	red wine vinegar	75 mL
1/3 cup	Worcestershire sauce	75 mL
1/4 tsp	dried oregano	1 mL
2 tsp	cayenne	5 mL
1/2 cup	brown sugar	125 mL
4 lb	meaty spareribs, cut into 4 servings	2 kg

1. Put garlic, onions, tomato sauce, bay leaves, vinegar and Worcestershire in a saucepan. Bring to a boil, then reduce heat and simmer, uncovered, for 30 minutes. Stir in the oregano, cayenne and brown sugar.

2. Preheat oven to 450° F (230° C).

3. Place ribs in roasting pan and cover with foil, but do not seal. Bake for 15 minutes. Reduce heat to 350° F (180° C) and pour sauce over the meat. Cover again loosely with foil and bake for 45 minutes, basting several times. Uncover and bake for 30 to 40 minutes longer, basting several times, until spareribs are richly glazed.

Serves 4

4
Pasta
& Grains

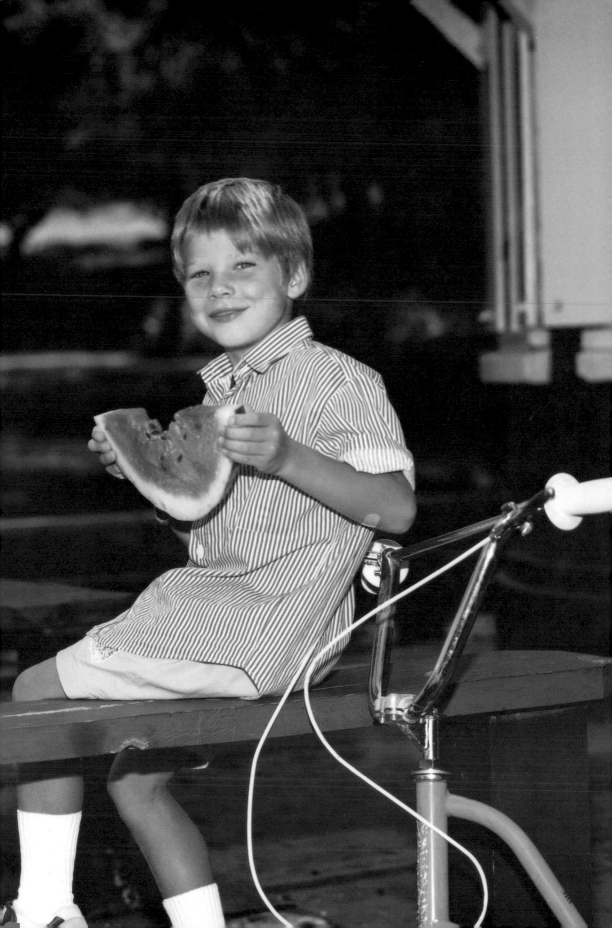

Barb Holland's Louisiana Sausage and Rice Supper

A delicious and quick dinner from microwave expert Barb Holland. Serve with a green salad and crusty bread.

2 tbsp	vegetable oil	25 mL
8 oz	smoked sausage, cut into 1/2-inch (1.25 cm) pieces	250 g
1	onion, chopped	1
1	green pepper, chopped	1
2	cloves garlic, finely chopped	2
1 cup	uncooked long-grain rice	250 mL
1 cup	tomato juice	250 mL
1 cup	chicken stock	250 mL
1 tsp	chili powder	5 mL
1/2 tsp	dried thyme	2 mL
1/2 tsp	dried oregano	2 mL
pinch	cayenne pepper	pinch
1	bay leaf	1
2 tbsp	chopped parsley	25 mL

MICROWAVE METHOD
In an 8-cup (2 L) microwavable dish, combine the sausage, onion, green pepper and garlic. Microwave, uncovered, at High (100%) for 3 to 4 minutes, or until vegetables are softened. Stir in the rice and microwave at High (100%) for 1 minute. Stir in the tomato juice, chicken stock and seasonings. Cover and microwave at High (100%) for 5 minutes. Microwave at Medium (50%) for 10 to 14 minutes, or until most of the liquid is absorbed. Remove the bay leaf, sprinkle with parsley and let stand, covered, for 10 minutes.

1. In a saucepan, heat oil over medium heat. Sauté sausage, onion, green pepper and garlic until vegetables are softened but not brown. Stir in rice and cook for 1 minute.

2. Stir in tomato juice, chicken stock and seasonings. Bring to a boil, cover and reduce heat. Simmer until rice is tender and liquid is absorbed, about 20 to 25 minutes. Remove bay leaf, sprinkle with parsley and serve.

Serves 3 to 4

Paola Scaravelli's Penne with Cheeses and Cream

Romano and Pecorino are cheeses made from ewe's milk, and are available in most Italian cheese shops. Pecorino is typical of central Italy, where pasture land is limited and of relatively poor quality, inadequate for cows but ideal for sheep.

This creamy rich sauce is ideal with short, stout pasta.

2 tbsp	butter	25 mL
1	large onion, thinly sliced	1
1/2 cup	water	125 mL
1/2 cup	peeled, seeded and finely chopped ripe tomatoes	125 mL
1 cup	whipping cream	250 mL
1 lb	uncooked penne or other stout pasta	500 g
1 cup	grated Gruyère cheese	250 mL
1/2 cup	freshly grated Romano or sharp Pecorino cheese	125 mL
	Pepper to taste	

1. Heat the butter in a saucepan on medium-low heat. Add the onion and sauté until golden, about 7 to 10 minutes.

2. Add the water and cook, uncovered, for 10 to 15 minutes, until the onion begins to disintegrate and the water has evaporated. Add the tomatoes and cream and simmer, uncovered for 5 minutes. Set aside.

3. Meanwhile, bring a large pot of salted water to a rapid boil. Add the pasta and cook until *al dente,* stirring occasionally with a wooden spoon. Drain and return the pasta to the pot.

4. Place the pot over low heat. Add the cream sauce and the grated cheeses. Blend well with a wooden spoon and cook for 1 minute. Transfer to a serving bowl, grind pepper over the pasta and serve immediately.

Serves 4

Spinach Fettuccine

1/4 cup	vegetable oil	50 mL
1	large onion, finely chopped	1
2	small cloves garlic, finely chopped	2
1/2 cup	diced ham	125 mL
1/2 cup	chopped mushrooms	125 mL
6	ripe tomatoes, peeled and finely chopped	6
1/2 tsp	dried thyme	2 mL
	Salt to taste	
1 lb	fresh spinach fettuccine	500 g
1/3 cup	grated Parmesan or Romano cheese	75 mL

Fresh pasta will take approximately 2 minutes to cook whereas dried will range from 8 to 10 minutes. *Al dente* **describes pasta which is cooked until tender but is still firm to the bite.**

1. In a large skillet, heat oil over medium heat. Cook onions until transparent. Add garlic, ham and mushrooms. Sauté for 10 minutes. Stir in tomatoes, thyme and salt and cook for 30 minutes.

2. Meanwhile, in a large saucepan, boil water with 2 tsp (10 mL) salt and 1 tbsp (15 mL) oil. Add fettuccine and cook until it is *al dente.* Drain well in a colander.

3. Just before serving, add fettuccine to skillet and toss well.

4. Sprinkle with Parmesan or Romano cheese and serve.

Serves 4

Spaghetti Fondue

A great healthy supper dish for kids. They love to dip bread and vegetables into the sauce. Provide lots of napkins as it's drippy. Serve with cubed bread or raw vegetables such as celery, carrots, zucchini, cauliflower and broccoli.

Basil, a popular Italian herb, is readily available fresh in the summer and fall. When substituting fresh herbs for dried use three times the amount. For example, 1 tsp (5 mL) dried herbs = 3 tsp (15 mL) fresh herbs.

1 tbsp	olive oil	15 mL
1 lb	ground chuck	500 g
2 cups	tomato sauce	500 mL
1 tsp	dried basil	5 mL
1 tsp	dried oregano	5 mL
1 tsp	chili powder	5 mL
1-1/2 cup	grated mozzarella cheese	375 mL
3 cups	grated Cheddar cheese	750 mL

1. In a skillet, heat oil over high heat and brown chuck.

2. Add the tomato sauce and seasonings. Simmer for 15 minutes.

3. Beat in the cheeses and simmer slowly until they melt, about 3 minutes.

Serves 4

Noodle Pudding

Serve with fried chicken, a green salad and crusty bread.
A great kid pleaser.

2 cups	slightly crushed cornflakes	500 mL
3/4 cup	granulated sugar	175 mL
1 tsp	cinnamon	5 mL
10 oz	medium noodles, cooked	300 g
2	eggs, lightly beaten	2
1/2 cup	orange juice	125 mL
1/4 cup	butter, melted and cooled	50 mL
1/2 tsp	vanilla	2 mL
1/2 tsp	salt	2 mL
2 cups	cherry pie filling	500 mL

1. Preheat oven to 350° F (180° C).

2. In a bowl, combine cornflakes, 1/4 cup (50 mL) sugar and cinnamon. Set aside.

3. In a large bowl, combine noodles with remaining 1/2 cup (125 mL) sugar, eggs, orange juice, melted butter, vanilla and salt.

4. In a buttered 11 x 7-inch (2 L) baking dish, layer half the noodle mixture. Spread the cherry pie filling over the noodles. Spread over the remaining half of the noodle mixture. Sprinkle on the cornflake topping.

5. Bake for 50 to 60 minutes, or until crusty on top and bubbly.

Serves 4 to 6

Leon Major's
Pasta and Asparagus

1 lb	asparagus, cut in pieces on diagonal	500 g
1/2 cup	olive oil	125 mL
1 tsp	finely chopped garlic	5 mL
1/4 cup	sun-dried tomatoes, cut into julienne strips	50 mL
2 tbsp	lemon juice	25 mL
1 tbsp	chopped fresh oregano, or 1 tsp (5 mL) dried oregano	15 mL
2 tbsp	chopped parsley	25 mL
1 lb	linguine, cooked	500 g
	Grated Parmesan cheese	

1. In a saucepan, cook asparagus in boiling salted water for 3 minutes. Drain and rinse in cold water.

2. In a large saucepan, heat the olive oil on medium heat. Add garlic and stir for 2 minutes. Add asparagus, tomatoes, lemon juice, oregano and parsley. Stir well.

3. Add cooked pasta and sprinkle with cheese.

Serves 4

Tuna Noodle Casserole Niçoise

A delightful update of a dependable favourite introduces the wonderful Niçoise ingredients to tuna and noodles – carrots, green beans, black olives, garlic and mustard.

3 cups	uncooked broad noodles	750 mL
1 tbsp	vegetable oil	15 mL
2	carrots, chopped	2
1 cup	sliced green beans	250 mL
1	small onion, chopped	1
1	clove garlic, finely chopped	1
1-1/4 cups	light cream	300 mL
1 tbsp	Dijon mustard	15 mL
1/2 tsp	dried oregano	2 mL
1/4 tsp	salt	1 mL
1	6-1/2-oz (184 g) can tuna, drained and flaked	1
1/4 cup	sliced pitted black olives	50 mL
1/4 cup	sliced almonds	50 mL

MICROWAVE METHOD
Cook the noodles on the stove. In a 6-cup (1.5 L) microwavable dish, combine the oil, carrots, beans, onion and garlic. Cover and cook at High (100%) for 3 to 4 minutes, or until the vegetables are tender. Stir in the cream, mustard, oregano, salt, tuna, olives and noodles. Sprinkle with the almonds and cook at Medium (50%) for 9 to 10 minutes, or until heated through.

1. Preheat oven to 350° F (180° C).

2. Cook noodles according to package directions. Drain and reserve.

3. Meanwhile, in a skillet, heat oil over medium heat. Sauté carrots, beans, onion and garlic until tender, about 4 minutes.

4. In a large bowl, whisk together cream, mustard, oregano and salt.

5. Stir in drained noodles, vegetables, tuna and olives.

6. Pour into greased 6-cup (1.5 L) baking dish.

7. Sprinkle with almonds. Bake for 25 minutes, or until sauce bubbles.

Serves 4

Elizabeth Baird's Spaghetti and Vegetable Frittata

A frittata is a firm omelette, which is cooked on top of the stove before being browned under the grill. It is not folded before being served.

Use any leftover pasta in this quick lunch dish. If you don't have leftover cooked spaghetti, you will need to cook approximately 6 oz (175 g) dried pasta.

2 tbsp	butter	25 mL
1	small onion, chopped	1
1/2 cup	chopped mushrooms	125 mL
1/2 cup	chopped green or red pepper	125 mL
1/2 cup	diced capocollo or ham	125 mL
6	eggs	6
2 tbsp	grated Parmesan cheese	25 mL
1 tbsp	chopped fresh parsley	15 mL
1/4 tsp	salt	1 mL
1/4 tsp	pepper	1 mL
2 cups	cooked spaghetti	500 mL

1. In a 12-inch (30 cm) nonstick skillet, melt 1 tbsp (15 mL) butter over medium heat.

2. Cook onion, mushrooms, green pepper and ham for 3 to 5 minutes, or until softened, stirring occasionally.

3. In a large bowl, whisk together eggs, cheese, half the parsley, onion mixture, salt and pepper.

4. Cut spaghetti into 2-inch (5 cm) lengths and stir into egg mixture.

5. In same skillet, melt remaining butter over medium heat, swirling to coat bottom and partway up sides.

6. Pour in egg mixture and cook, without stirring, for 3 to 5 minutes, or until bottom is golden and most of the egg mixture has set.

7. Invert frittata onto plate and slide back into skillet, cooked side up. Continue cooking for 3 to 4 minutes longer, or until golden.

8. Garnish with remaining parsley. Serve hot or warm, sliced in wedges.

Serves 4

Pasta with Sausages and Zucchini

2 tbsp	olive oil	25 mL
3	zucchini, diced	3
1	red pepper, diced	1
1	onion, chopped	1
1 lb	Polish sausage, diced	500 g
1-1/2 cups	drained canned tomatoes	375 mL
	Salt and pepper to taste	
1 lb	fettuccine, cooked	500 g

Sausages are smoked to give them a unique taste, ranging from mild to highly smoked. The heavier the smoke, the darker and more full-flavoured the sausage will be. Chorizo, pepperoni and Polish sausage are three common varieties of smoked sausage.

Dried pasta is usually used with sauces that are spicy or on the heavy side, such as tomato-based sauces. Fresh pasta is used for delicate, creamy sauces where you want the pasta to absorb the creamy liquids.

1. In a skillet, heat oil on medium heat. Sauté zucchini, peppers and onions until softened, about 2 minutes.

2. Add sausage and tomatoes. Cook together for 10 minutes. Season with salt and pepper. Serve over cooked fettuccine.

Serves 4

Chickpea and Potato Casserole

A hearty side dish served with lamb or a vegetable main dish served with a salad.

Chickpeas are also called garbanzo beans. They have a nutty, earthy taste and are high in trace elements, including magnesium and zinc. They are also a very good source of iron.

1/3 cup	olive oil	75 mL
2 cups	sliced onions	500 mL
6 cups	thickly sliced new or red potatoes	1.5 L
1/3 cup	all-purpose flour	75 mL
1	19-oz (540 mL) can chickpeas, undrained	1
2 cups	chopped tomatoes	500 mL
3 tbsp	chopped parsley	45 mL
4	cloves garlic, minced	4
1 tbsp	dried oregano	15 mL
2 tsp	ground cinnamon	10 mL
	Salt and pepper to taste	

Topping

3 cups	plain yogurt	750 mL
3	egg yolks	3
1/2 cup	grated Parmesan or Romano cheese	125 mL
1 tbsp	all-purpose flour	15 mL

1. Preheat oven to 350 F° (180° C).

2. In a skillet, heat oil on high heat. Add onions and potatoes and cook, scraping the bottom frequently, until onions are softened, about 2 minutes. Reduce the heat to medium and add the flour. Stir well and add the chickpeas with their liquid, tomatoes, parsley, garlic, oregano, cinnamon, salt and pepper. Simmer for 10 minutes.

3. Turn mixture into a 13 x 9-inch (3.5 L) casserole.

4. To prepare topping, in a bowl, whisk together the yogurt, egg yolks, cheese and flour. Pour evenly over the vegetable mixture. Bake until lightly browned, about 15 to 20 minutes. Let cool for 15 minutes before serving or, better yet, let cool completely, then reheat at 325° F (160° C) for about 20 minutes.

Serves 10 to 12

David Wood's Polenta

Serve this with braised beef ribs and a green salad.

3 cups	water	750 mL
3/4 cup	yellow cornmeal	175 mL
1/2 tsp	salt	2 mL
1/4 cup	butter	50 mL
1/4 cup	grated Parmesan cheese	50 mL

Polenta is an Italian cornmeal side dish with a texture similar to cream of wheat. It can be served as a substitute for potatoes or rice. As polenta cools, it becomes firmer in texture and can be cut into squares and sautéed or deep-fried, or it can be baked in a sauce.

1. In a saucepan, bring the water to a boil over high heat. Add the cornmeal and salt and return to a boil, stirring constantly.

2. Lower heat to medium and cook, stirring constantly, for about 15 minutes, until the mixture is smooth and quite thick. Stir in the butter. Just before serving, stir in the Parmesan cheese.

Serves 4

Magnificent Muesli

This gourmet breakfast was a big hit with the recipe testers!
Muesli is a combination of grains and fruit, often sweetened with honey.
You can also add seeds and nuts to this recipe if you wish.

Rolled oats are higher in protein than most grains and are a good source of B vitamins.

1/2 cup	butter	125 mL
1-1/2 cups	rolled oats	375 mL
1/4 cup	honey	50 mL
1-1/2 cups	cornflakes	375 mL
3	pears, cored and chopped	3
2	apples, cored and chopped	2
2 cups	raspberries	500 mL
2 tbsp	lemon juice	25 mL
2	bananas	2
1/3 cup	milk	75 mL
3 tbsp	mascarpone or cream cheese	45 mL

1. In a skillet on medium heat, heat butter. Sauté oats. Stir in honey. Cool. Add cornflakes and mix well, trying not to crush flakes. Add pears, apples and raspberries to mixture along with lemon juice.

2. In a blender, make the sauce by puréeing bananas with 3 tbsp (45 mL) milk. Add mascarpone and 3 tbsp (45 mL) more milk. Blend. Add a little more milk if too thick and a little more mascarpone if too thin.

3. Divide muesli among four bowls. Pour sauce over and serve.

Serves 4

Bulgur Pilaf

To obtain the best texture, use the exact amounts of stock and bulgur called for. For variation, add chopped green pepper, chopped nuts, grated carrots or sliced ripe olives. This recipe doubles nicely.

2 tbsp	butter	25 mL
1/2 cup	chopped celery	125 mL
1	onion, chopped	1
1/2 cup	sliced mushrooms	125 mL
1 cup	uncooked bulgur	250 mL
1/4 tsp	dried dill	1 mL
1/4 tsp	dried oregano	1 mL
1/2 tsp	salt	2 mL
1/4 tsp	pepper	1 mL
2 cups	chicken stock	500 mL
1 tbsp	chopped parsley	15 mL
2 tbsp	chopped pimento	25 mL

Bulgur is Middle Eastern cracked wheat, made from wheat berries that have been crushed, cooked and dried. It has a fine nutty flavour, and can be purchased at health food stores.

Bulgur is interchangeable with cracked wheat.

Cracked wheat is made from wheat berries that have been cracked, then coarsely milled.

1. In a large skillet, melt butter. Add celery, onions, mushrooms and bulgur. Cook, stirring, until tender, about 2 minutes.

2. Add seasonings and stock. Cover and bring to a boil. Reduce heat and simmer for 15 minutes.

3. Stir in parsley and pimento just before serving.

Serves 4

Rice and Beans

Wonderfully easy to prepare, the vegetable and bean sauce can be made while the rice is cooking. With the addition of a salad, it's a nutritious, tasty vegetarian meal without much fuss.

Brown rice is higher in fibre and B vitamins. White rice has had the bran removed during processing. Quick-cook rice or instant rice is the least nutritious.

2 cups	water	500 mL
1 cup	uncooked white or brown rice	250 mL
1 tbsp	vegetable oil	15 mL
1	large onion, chopped	1
3	cloves garlic, chopped	3
1	zucchini, cut in 1-inch (2.5 cm) cubes	1
1	green pepper, cut in 1-inch (2.5 cm) cubes	1
2	tomatoes, diced	2
1 tsp	dried basil	5 mL
1/2 tsp	dried oregano	2 mL
1	19-oz (540 mL) can chickpeas or kidney beans, drained	1
	Pepper to taste	
1 cup	grated Cheddar cheese	250 mL

1. In a saucepan, bring water to a rolling boil. Add rice. Reduce heat, cover and simmer for 20 minutes. (If using brown rice, simmer for 35 minutes.) Keep the pot covered while preparing vegetable and bean sauce.

2. Heat oil in a large skillet on medium heat. Add onion and garlic and sauté until soft, about 2 minutes.

3. Add zucchini, peppers, tomatoes, basil and oregano. Cover pan and simmer for about 5 minutes, or until vegetables are cooked.

4. Add chickpeas or kidney beans and cook, stirring occasionally, until mixture is hot. Season with pepper.

5. Serve over hot rice and sprinkle the cheese on top.

Serves 4 to 6

Barb Holland's Spicy Macaroni and Cheddar Cheese

A zippy departure from the classic macaroni and cheese from Toronto Star *columnist Barb Holland. Try interesting pasta shapes such as rotini, penne, ziti or medium shells.*

8 oz	rotini, penne, ziti or medium shells	250 g
2 tbsp	butter	25 mL
1	onion, chopped	1
1	fresh hot pepper, chopped	1
3 tbsp	all-purpose flour	45 mL
1/2 tsp	salt	2 mL
1/4 tsp	pepper	1 mL
2 cups	milk	500 mL
1-1/2 cups	grated old Cheddar cheese	375 mL
1 tsp	Dijon mustard	5 mL
1/2 tsp	Worcestershire sauce	2 mL

MICROWAVE METHOD
Cook the pasta on the stove. Meanwhile, in an 8-cup (2 L) microwavable dish, combine the butter, onion, and hot pepper. Microwave, uncovered, at High (100%) for 2 to 4 minutes, or until vegetables are softened. Stir in the flour, salt and pepper and microwave at High (100%) for 40 to 60 seconds. Gradually stir in the milk. Microwave, uncovered, at High (100%) for 6 to 8 minutes, until the mixture comes to a boil and thickens. Stir every 2 minutes. Stir in the cheese until melted, then add the mustard and Worcestershire. Drain the pasta well and transfer to a warm dish. Pour the cheese sauce over and toss well.

1. In a large pot, cook pasta in salted boiling water until *al dente* (tender but firm). While pasta is cooking, make the sauce.

2. In a saucepan, melt butter over medium heat. Add onion and hot pepper and cook until softened but not browned. Stir in flour, salt and pepper and cook briefly.

3. Gradually stir in milk and cook, stirring constantly, until mixture comes to a boil and thickens. Reduce heat and simmer for a few minutes. Stir in cheese until melted, then mustard and Worcestershire sauce. Remove from heat.

4. Drain pasta well and transfer to a warmed bowl or pasta dish. Pour sauce over and mix well.

Serves 4

Lentils and Rice

For a main-dish casserole, add 2 cups (500 mL)
grated Swiss cheese to this recipe.

Brown rice still has a protective kernel, and therefore must be cooked for longer than white rice, which has had the outer kernel removed. Brown rice is nutritionally superior to white rice, due to its higher fibre and vitamin B content.

2-2/3 cups	chicken stock	650 mL
3/4 cup	dried lentils	175 mL
3/4 cup	chopped onions	175 mL
1/2 cup	uncooked brown rice	125 mL
4 oz	mushrooms, sliced	125 g
1/2 tsp	dried basil	2 mL
1/4 tsp	salt	1 mL
1/4 tsp	dried oregano	1 mL
1/4 tsp	dried thyme	1 mL
1	clove garlic, minced	1
pinch	pepper	pinch

1. Preheat oven to 350° F (180° C).

2. In a bowl, combine chicken stock, lentils, onions, rice, mushrooms and seasonings. Turn into an ungreased 6-cup (1.5 L) casserole.

3. Bake, covered, for 1 to 1-1/2 hours, or until lentils and rice are tender.

Serves 4

5
Vegetables & Salads

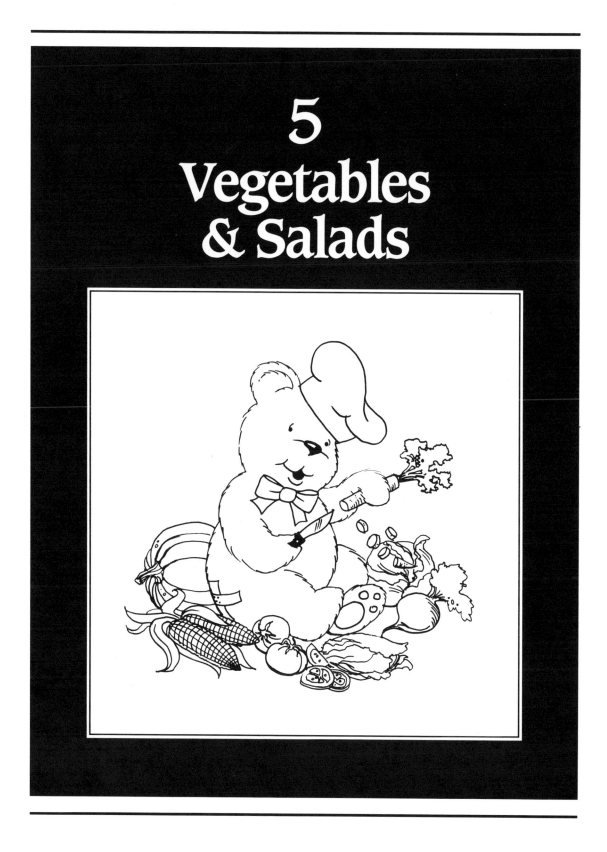

Red Cabbage

1	red cabbage, shredded	1
3/4 cup	cider vinegar	175 mL
1/3 cup	granulated sugar	75 mL
1-1/4 tsp	salt	6 mL
1 tbsp	vegetable oil	15 mL
6	slices bacon, chopped	6
2	apples, cored and chopped	2
1	onion, chopped	1
4	whole cloves	4
4	cloves garlic, minced	4
2	bay leaves	2
8	whole peppercorns	8
1/2 tsp	ground allspice	2 mL
3 tbsp	red wine	45 mL

Cabbage is packed full of many vitamins and minerals. It is a good source of vitamin C. Cabbage, belonging to the brassica family of vegetables, is thought to help reduce the risk of several forms of cancer.

1. In a large bowl, toss cabbage with vinegar, sugar and salt. Let sit for 30 minutes.

2. In a heavy 12-cup (3 L) casserole, melt vegetable oil on medium heat. Add bacon and sauté until brown.

3. Add apples and onions and cook for 5 minutes.

4. Add cabbage mixture, cloves, garlic, bay leaves, peppercorns, allspice and red wine. Cover and simmer for 1 hour. Uncover and simmer for 30 minutes, or until sauce is thick and cabbage is tender.

Serves 6 to 8

Lucy Waverman's Zucchini Linguine

This is a good way to use up large zucchini, when they are plentiful.
From Lucy Waverman's Seasonal Canadian Cookbook *(Harper Collins).*

2	large zucchini	2
2 tbsp	olive oil	25 mL
1 tbsp	butter	15 mL
1	clove garlic, finely chopped	1
	Salt and pepper to taste	

1. Using shredding disc of a food processor or a hand grater, grate zucchini into long shreds.

2. In a large skillet, heat oil and butter on medium-high heat. Add zucchini and garlic. Sauté until zucchini is limp. Season with salt and pepper.

Serves 6

Make-Ahead Mashed Potatoes

This dish can be prepared the day before and refrigerated overnight before being baked.

5	large baking potatoes, peeled	5
4 oz	cream cheese, at room temperature	125 g
1/2 cup	sour cream	125 mL
2	green onions, chopped	2
1/2 tsp	salt	2 mL
pinch	pepper	pinch
1 tbsp	butter	15 mL

1. Preheat oven to 350° F (180° C).

2. In a saucepan, boil potatoes in salted water until tender.

3. Drain potatoes and mash very well. Beat in remaining ingredients. Place in a 13 x 9-inch (3.5 L) baking dish.

4. Bake, covered, for 30 minutes, or until hot.

Serves 6

There are many different types of potatoes. Round new potatoes have a lower starch content than regular potatoes and are best for boiling and potato salads. Elongated oval potatoes such as Russet and Idaho have a floury texture and are best for baking, mashing and french fries.

Potatoes have been a dietary staple for centuries because they are high in complex carbohydrates and potassium. If they are eaten unpeeled, they are also an excellent source of fibre. The calories in potato dishes mainly come from the butter and milk; if you are worried about calories, eat them unadorned.

Orange
Sweet Potatoes

Although they taste sweet, sweet potatoes have the same calorie count as regular potatoes. They contain a great deal of vitamin A. Do not refrigerate them, because the humidity will encourage rapid spoilage. Try to use them within one week of buying.

4	sweet potatoes	4
1/2 cup	brown sugar	125 mL
1/4 cup	white wine	50 mL
1 tsp	cornstarch	5 mL
1/2 cup	orange juice	125 mL
pinch	salt	pinch

1. In a large saucepan, boil sweet potatoes in salted water until just tender. Peel and cut into slices 1/2 inch (1.25 cm) thick. Layer in a greased 8-cup (2 L) ovenproof casserole.

2. Preheat oven to 350° F (180° C).

3. In a saucepan on medium heat, melt the brown sugar, then add wine.

4. In a small bowl, dissolve cornstarch in orange juice. Add to the sugar and wine mixture. Add salt and simmer for 5 minutes. Pour over the sweet potatoes.

5. Bake for 30 minutes, covered, then 30 minutes, uncovered, or until sweet potatoes are sticky.

Serves 4

Spinach Pecan Bake

3	10-oz (300 g) packages spinach, chopped	3
1/4 cup	butter	50 mL
1/2 cup	finely chopped onions	125 mL
1 cup	light cream	250 mL
2/3 cup	fresh breadcrumbs	150 mL
1/2 cup	chopped pecans	125 mL
1 tsp	salt	5 mL
1/2 tsp	nutmeg	2 mL
pinch	pepper	pinch
2 tbsp	butter	25 mL

When purchasing fresh spinach, look for bright-green leaves that are not wilted. The spinach must be washed thoroughly to dislodge the sand and dirt. Spinach exudes water and will turn slimy if it is stored in a plastic bag.

1. Preheat oven to 350° F (180° C).

2. Wash spinach thoroughly, and cook on medium heat for 5 minutes, or until wilted. Drain well.

3. In a skillet on medium heat, heat 1/4 cup (50 mL) butter. Sauté onions until softened. Add spinach, cream, 1/3 cup (75 mL) breadcrumbs, pecans, salt, nutmeg and pepper. Mix well.

4. Place in a buttered 6-cup (1.5 L) casserole dish.

5. Sprinkle remaining breadcrumbs over the spinach. Dot with remaining butter.

6. Bake for 30 minutes, or until heated through.

Serves 6

Spinach Mashed Potatoes

6	potatoes, peeled	6
1 cup	chopped cooked spinach	250 mL
1/2 cup	milk	125 mL
2 tbsp	butter	25 mL
	Salt, pepper and nutmeg to taste	

For a more nutritious salad choose spinach instead of lettuce. It is higher in vitamins A and C, also in iron and fibre.

1. In a saucepan, cook potatoes in boiling salted water until tender. Drain and mash. Keep warm.

2. Meanwhile, in another saucepan, cook spinach in milk over low heat until hot. Add spinach/milk mixture to mashed potatoes along with butter. Whisk together. Season with salt, pepper and nutmeg. Serve immediately.

Serves 6

Scalloped Apples and Turnip

This is great served with roast turkey or chicken.

1	large turnip, peeled and diced	1
	Salt and pepper to taste	
1/2 cup	brown sugar	125 mL
1/2 cup	all-purpose flour	125 mL
1/2 cup	butter	125 mL
6	apples, peeled and sliced	6

1. Place turnip in saucepan and cover with cold water. Bring to boil and boil until tender, about 10 minutes. Drain well and mash. Season with salt and pepper.

2. Preheat oven to 350° F (180° C).

3. In a bowl, combine brown sugar and flour. Cut in butter, mixing until mixture is crumbly.

4. In a buttered 8-cup (2 L) baking dish, layer half the mashed turnip. Cover turnip with half the sliced apples and half the brown sugar mixture. Cover with the remaining apples, turnip, and brown sugar.

5. Bake until topping is bubbly and brown, approximately 30 minutes. Do not overcook, or the sugar will burn.

Serves 6

Rutabagas and turnips are actually two different vegetables, though in Canada rutabagas are often sold as turnips. Turnips are mild-tasting, white root vegetables with a purple tinge to the skin; the larger rutabagas have a waxed brown skin and yellow flesh.

Norman Jewison's Maple-Glazed Squash

Norman Jewison uses maple syrup that he collects from his own maple farm in Caledon, just north of Toronto. A great dish served with Thanksgiving turkey.

2	small acorn or pepper squash	2
1/2 tsp	salt	2 mL
1/4 cup	butter, melted	50 mL
1/2 cup	maple syrup	125 mL
1/2 tsp	finely grated orange rind	2 mL

1. Preheat oven to 375° F (190° C).

2. Trim ends from squash. Cut each squash into three rings and remove seeds.

3. Place squash in baking dish, sprinkle with salt and drizzle with butter. Bake until almost tender, approximately 45 minutes.

4. In a saucepan, combine maple syrup and orange rind. Bring to a boil, reduce heat and simmer until thickened, about 3 to 4 minutes. Pour over squash and continue baking until squash is tender, about 10 minutes.

Serves 6

Lucy Waverman's Steamed Vegetables with Lemon Sauce

Remember to peel the rough outer skin of the broccoli stalks so that the vegetable cooks evenly.

1 tsp	salt	5 mL
1	small bunch broccoli, cut into florets	1
1	small head cauliflower, cut into florets	1
	Juice of 1 lemon	
3 tbsp	butter	45 mL
1 tbsp	finely chopped fresh dill	15 mL

1. Fill a large pot with 1 inch (2.5 cm) water. Add salt. Bring water to a boil.

2. Peel broccoli stalks. Place broccoli and cauliflower in a steamer basket and place the basket in the pot. Cover and steam until the vegetables are crisp-tender, about 5 to 8 minutes.

3. Meanwhile, heat lemon juice in a skillet over high heat. Boil until it is reduced to 1 tbsp (15 mL). Reduce heat to low and whisk in butter and dill. Pour sauce over the vegetables.

Serves 6

Broccoli Pudding

This can actually be eaten as a meal in itself or as a side dish with chicken or fish. It receives rave reviews at brunches, too.

Cottage cheese is an economical source of protein and is low in calories.

6	eggs, beaten	6
1/3 cup	all-purpose flour	75 mL
2 cups	cottage cheese	500 mL
1/2 cup	butter, melted	125 mL
1 cup	grated Cheddar cheese	250 mL
1	bunch broccoli, lightly steamed and chopped	1
2	carrots, grated	2
	Salt and pepper to taste	

1. Preheat oven to 350° F (180° C).

2. In a large bowl, mix together the eggs, flour, cottage cheese, butter, 1/2 cup (125 mL) cheese, broccoli and carrots. Add salt and pepper to taste.

3. Pour mixture into a well-greased 12 x 8-inch (3 L) baking dish. Sprinkle remaining Cheddar cheese on top.

4. Bake for 1 hour.

Serves 6

Baked Eggplant

This dish may seem too simple to be good, but it is even better than that; it is truly outstanding. The tomato sauce, oregano and garlic draw out the eggplant's unique taste. For those who like eggplant, there may be no better way to prepare it.

6	small young eggplants, washed and cut in half lengthwise	6
2	cloves garlic, minced	2
1/2 cup	tomato sauce	125 mL
1 tsp	dried oregano	5 mL
1/2 tsp	salt	2 mL
1/4 tsp	pepper	1 mL
3 tbsp	olive oil	45 mL

Before using eggplant, slice it and sprinkle the slices lightly with salt. Place in a colander and let sit for 30 minutes to draw out the bitter juices. Pat dry before using.

1. Preheat oven to 375° F (190° C).

2. Cut cross-hatches on the skin of the eggplants, about 1/2 inch (1.25 cm) apart and 1/4 inch (5 mm) deep. Rub the garlic into the slits.

3. Place eggplants cut side up on a baking sheet. Spread tomato sauce on each eggplant half, sprinkle with oregano, salt and pepper and drizzle with the olive oil.

4. Bake for 35 to 40 minutes, until the eggplants are tender and cooked through. To test, plunge a cake tester or toothpick into the centre of an eggplant. If cooked, the tester will slide in easily. Remove from the oven and serve hot.

Serves 6

Tomato-Zucchini Vinaigrette

This is a wonderful way to serve tomatoes and zucchini at the peak of their season. You may decide to make the recipe with tomatoes only, especially when they are in great supply from your own or neighbouring gardens. Children really enjoy the tangy flavour. On a hot summer evening, adding the chickpeas could make this salad a meal in itself, served with fresh crusty bread.

3	ripe tomatoes, diced	3
1	large zucchini, sliced	1
1/2	small onion, diced	1/2
1/2 tsp	dried oregano	2 mL
1/2 tsp	dried basil	2 mL
1	clove garlic, minced	1
1/2 tsp	Worcestershire sauce	2 mL
2 tbsp	white vinegar	25 mL
2 cups	cooked chickpeas (optional)	500 mL

1. In a bowl, combine all ingredients and toss. Refrigerate and cover until serving.

Serves 6

Linda Lundstrom's
Baked Barbecued Potatoes

These are great for the barbecue because they can be put on as soon as you start your barbecue, and by the time the coals are ready for the rest of your meal these potatoes can be moved to the side to finish cooking. Serve them with sour cream or plain yogurt with chives on top.

12	potatoes	12
1/2 tsp	salt	2 mL
1/2 tsp	pepper	2 mL
1 tsp	dried tarragon	5 mL
1 tsp	cumin seeds	5 mL
1/2 cup	butter	125 mL

1. Wash potatoes. Leave skins on and cut into 1/4-inch (5 mm) slices. Place in a bowl and sprinkle with salt, pepper, tarragon and cumin seeds.

2. Place a large sheet of wide heavy-duty aluminum foil shiny side up on the counter. Mound potatoes in an oblong shape in the middle. Dot butter on top. Fold up package and seal securely.

3. Place on barbecue immediately after it is lit and leave on for 30 to 45 minutes, or until potatoes are tender.

Serves 10

Cauliflower Cheese Pie

A potato crust filled with cheesy cauliflower makes a great vegetarian main course served with a salad. It's a sure-fire kid-pleaser, too.

Nutmeg is the fruit of a tropical tree. It can be bought whole (which needs to be grated) or ground. Excellent with all milk puddings, and for a change, try it sprinkled sparingly on your roast beef.

Crust

2 cups	grated raw potato	500 mL
1/2 cup	grated onion	125 mL
1/2 tsp	salt	2 mL
1	egg, beaten	1
	Salt and pepper to taste	

Filling

3 tbsp	butter	45 mL
1	clove garlic, finely chopped	1
1 cup	finely chopped onion	250 mL
1	head cauliflower, broken into small florets	1
1 tsp	dried basil	5 mL
1/2 tsp	dried thyme	2 mL
1-1/2 cups	grated old Cheddar cheese	375 mL
2	eggs, beaten	2
1/4 cup	milk	50 mL
1 tbsp	chopped parsley	15 mL
1 tbsp	grated Parmesan cheese	15 mL
pinch	nutmeg	pinch
	Salt and pepper to taste	
	Paprika	

1. Sprinkle grated potato and onion with salt and set to drain in sieve for about 15 minutes. Squeeze out excess water and place in bowl. Add beaten egg, salt and pepper.

2. Preheat oven to 425° F (220° C).

3. Generously oil 9-inch (23 cm) pie pan and dust with flour. Press potato mixture evenly into the pan so that it forms a shell.

4. Bake for 45 minutes, until browned. Brush crust with oil during the last 15 minutes of baking to crisp it.

5. Reduce oven temperature to 350° F (180° C).

6. In a large skillet, heat butter on medium heat. Add garlic and onions and cook until soft. Add cauliflower and dried herbs and continue to cook for about 25 minutes, just until cauliflower is tender, stirring occasionally.

7. Line the prepared crust with half the Cheddar, then half the cauliflower mixture; repeat with a second layer.

8. In a bowl, combine eggs, milk, parsley, Parmesan and nutmeg. Add salt and pepper. Pour over the cauliflower and dust the top with the paprika.

9. Bake for about 45 minutes, until the cauliflower is cooked and the top is crusty.

Serves 6

Liquid Measures

1 cup = 240 mL	1 litre = 4-1/2 cups
1/2 cup = 120 mL	500 mL = 2-1/4 cups
1 tbsp = 15 mL	100 mL = 6-1/2 tbsp

Lucy Waverman's Stir-Fried Asparagus

When buying asparagus, look for straight firm stalks with closed heads. Snap off the woody bottom ends and peel thick stalks before using. Cook the asparagus until the stalks are just tender but still have some texture. Overcooked asparagus becomes mushy and tasteless. Store asparagus in the refrigerator wrapped in damp paper towels.

To turn this into a complete meal, add about 8 oz (250 g) slivered chicken, flank steak or pork to the wok and cook for 2 minutes before adding the asparagus. Use thin asparagus, if available, to avoid peeling. If you do not have sesame oil, sprinkle with sesame seeds.

2 lb	asparagus	1 kg
2 tbsp	vegetable oil	25 mL
1 tbsp	finely chopped fresh ginger	15 mL
1/4 cup	chicken stock or water	50 mL
1 tbsp	soy sauce	15 mL
1 tsp	oriental sesame oil	5 mL

1. Slice asparagus into 1-inch (2.5 cm) lengths.

2. Heat oil in a skillet or wok on high heat. Add ginger and stir-fry for 30 seconds.

3. Add asparagus and stir-fry for 1 minute. Pour in chicken stock, cover pan and let asparagus steam for 2 minutes, or until crisp-tender.

4. Remove cover and sprinkle with soy sauce and sesame oil.

Serves 4

Greek Salad

1/4 cup	olive oil	50 mL
1/4 cup	red wine vinegar	50 mL
1 tbsp	lemon juice	15 mL
1 tsp	dried oregano	5 mL
	Salt and pepper to taste	
3	large tomatoes, cut into chunks	3
1	large red onion, cut into strips	1
1	large zucchini, sliced	1
12	black olives	12
1 cup	feta cheese, cut into chunks	250 mL
1	large red pepper, cut into strips	1
	Romaine or iceberg lettuce	

Use a high-quality olive oil when making salads. Virgin olive oil is cold pressed, green in colour, and contains no additives. Use it on delicate salads where the taste of the oil comes through. Olive oil should be stored in a dark container or cupboard because it will eventually spoil if exposed to the light.

1. In a small bowl, whisk together oil, vinegar, lemon juice, oregano, salt and pepper.

2. Combine tomatoes, onion, zucchini, olives, feta cheese and red pepper in a large bowl. Pour the dressing over and toss. Serve on a bed of lettuce.

Serves 4

Hot German Potato Salad

Serve this salad with pork chops or sausages.
Leftovers can be reheated in the oven or microwave.

When making potato salad, always dress the potatoes while they are still warm; they will absorb the dressing better.

3	strips bacon	3
1	small onion, diced	1
1	small green pepper, diced	1
1 cup	mayonnaise	250 mL
1 tbsp	white vinegar	15 mL
2 tbsp	water	25 mL
1 tbsp	Worcestershire sauce	15 mL
1/2 tsp	dry mustard	2 mL
3 cups	sliced cooked potatoes	750 mL
3	hard-cooked eggs, chopped	3
1/2 cup	chopped celery	125 mL
1/4 cup	chopped dill pickles	50 mL

1. In a large skillet on medium heat, fry bacon until crisp, then remove, crumble and reserve.

2. Add onion and green pepper to the skillet and sauté until tender, about 3 minutes.

3. Add mayonnaise, vinegar, water, Worcestershire and dry mustard. Cook over low heat for a few minutes until heated thoroughly. Add potatoes, eggs, celery and pickles. Toss together, making sure potatoes are well coated. Serve warm, sprinkled with bacon.

Serves 8

Fresh Fruit Salad

1/2 cup	sour cream	125 mL
1/2 cup	mayonnaise	125 mL
1 tbsp	poppy seeds	15 mL
1 tbsp	sesame seeds	15 mL
1 tbsp	granulated sugar	15 mL
1 tsp	lemon juice	5 mL
4 cups	lettuce, torn into bite-sized pieces	1 L
4 cups	fresh fruit (strawberries, pineapple, kiwi, etc.), cut into bite-sized pieces	1 L

Poppy seeds are small, deep blue seeds of a type of poppy which have a mild but distinctive flavour. They can be sprinkled on bread, pastries or cakes.

1. In a bowl, combine sour cream, mayonnaise, poppy seeds, sesame seeds, sugar and lemon juice.

2. Place lettuce on plates. Place the fruit on top of lettuce. Drizzle the dressing over and serve immediately.

Serves 4

Summer Noodle Salad

A light, nutritious and very easy noodle salad that both adults and children love. It can be made several hours ahead. Sprinkle toasted sesame seeds or sunflower seeds on the salad before serving, if you wish.

Rice vinegar is a very mild vinegar made from fermented rice; if it is unavailable, use cider vinegar.

1/2 cup	peanut butter	125 mL
1/3 cup	hot water	75 mL
1/3 cup	soy sauce	75 mL
1/4 cup	rice vinegar or cider vinegar	50 mL
2 tbsp	oriental sesame oil	25 mL
	Tabasco sauce to taste	
1 lb	uncooked angel hair pasta	500 g
4	green onions, chopped	4
2 cups	chopped cucumber	500 mL

1. In a large bowl, mix together peanut butter, water, soy sauce, vinegar, sesame oil and Tabasco.

2. In a saucepan, boil pasta in salted water until *al dente.* Drain and rinse with cold water. Immediately toss noodles in the sauce.

3. Add green onions and cucumber and toss again. Serve at room temperature.

Serves 4

Summer
Vegetable Salad

A light and very easy salad. It's especially good on hot days and when fresh basil is easily available. Any vegetables can be used. The vegetables can also be blanched before using, if preferred.

1	bunch broccoli, cut into florets	1
1	head cauliflower, cut into florets	1
4	carrots, thinly sliced	4
1 cup	loosely packed fresh basil leaves	250 mL
1/3 cup	vegetable oil	75 mL
1/3 cup	olive oil	75 mL
1/2 cup	rice vinegar	125 mL
1/2 cup	lemon juice	125 mL
8	lettuce leaves	8

1. In a large bowl, mix together broccoli, cauliflower and carrots.

2. In a food processor or blender, combine basil, oils, vinegar and lemon juice until the basil is finely chopped.

3. Pour over vegetables, toss, cover and refrigerate for one day.

4. Serve salad on lettuce leaves.

Serves 8

Romaine and Strawberry Salad

Chinese cabbage is similar to celery in texture, but it has a sweeter taste. Look for pale heads since they have a more delicate flavour.

1	bunch Romaine lettuce	1
2	bunches Chinese cabbage, sliced	500 mL
2 cups	sliced strawberries	500 mL
2 cups	blueberries	500 mL
1	small red onion, thinly sliced	1
1/3 cup	olive oil	75 mL
1 tbsp	wine vinegar	15 mL
1 tbsp	lemon juice	15 mL
1/2 tsp	granulated sugar	2 mL
1/4 tsp	salt	1 mL
1/4 tsp	pepper	1 mL

1. Tear lettuce into bite-sized pieces. Place lettuce and cabbage in a large bowl.

2. Arrange strawberries, blueberries and onions over greens.

3. In a jar, combine remaining ingredients and shake well. Pour over the salad and serve immediately.

Serves 6

Cole Slaw

This is a classic sweet and tart Jewish cole slaw; the recipe comes from a great Jewish cook, Pearl Goodman. It keeps for one week in the refrigerator.

1	head cabbage, thinly sliced	1
4	carrots, thinly sliced	4
1	green pepper, thinly sliced	1
1	red pepper, thinly sliced	1
1	red onion, thinly sliced	1
2/3 cup	vegetable oil	150 mL
1/2 cup	white vinegar	125 mL
1/4 cup	lemon juice	50 mL
1/3 cup	granulated sugar	75 mL
1 tbsp	salt	15 mL
2 tsp	pepper	10 mL
1	clove garlic, minced	1

Carrots – in common with other orange and red vegetables such as pumpkins, red peppers and tomatoes – are a strong source of vitamin A (carotene).

1. In a bowl, combine cabbage, carrots, green and red peppers and red onion.

2. In a jar, combine remaining ingredients and shake well.

3. Pour dressing over the salad and let sit for a couple of hours. Toss well before serving.

Serves 8 to 10

Barbara Frum's Oriental Salad

Use farfalle (butterfly) pasta or fusilli for a pretty look.
This is a great summer buffet dish.

Snow peas should be trimmed by pulling off the little stem and string along one side of the pod. They are available year round and are best eaten raw, stir-fried or steamed. Sugar snaps are a seasonal pea that mature with a tender, edible pod; they can be eaten whole, but they should be trimmed like snow peas.

1	zucchini, diced	1
1	bunch broccoli, cut into florets	1
8 oz	snow peas	250 g
1	small head cauliflower, cut into florets	1
1 cup	sliced water chestnuts	250 mL
1 lb	pasta, cooked	500 mL
8 oz	cooked baby shrimp	250 g
1	mango, sliced	1
1-1/2 cups	mayonnaise	375 mL
1 tbsp	soy sauce	15 mL
2 tsp	oriental sesame oil	10 mL
1/4 cup	rice vinegar	50 mL
1 tbsp	finely chopped ginger root	15 mL
2 tbsp	chopped fresh coriander	25 mL

1. Combine vegetables, pasta, shrimp and mango in a large bowl.

2. Combine all remaining ingredients and pour over salad. Serve immediately.

Serves 8

6
Muffins &
Quickbreads

Blueberry Muffins

2 cups	plain yogurt	500 mL
2 tsp	baking soda	10 mL
1-1/2 cups	brown sugar	375 mL
1 cup	vegetable oil	250 mL
2	eggs	2
2 cups	bran	500 mL
2 tsp	vanilla	10 mL
2 cups	all-purpose flour	500 mL
4 tsp	baking powder	20 mL
1/2 tsp	salt	2 mL
1 cup	fresh or frozen unsweetened blueberries	250 mL

When making muffins, make sure you don't overmix the batter, because it will deflate. Don't worry about a few lumps. When baking, use paper muffin cups, or grease the muffin pan with butter or oil.

1. Preheat oven to 350° F (180° C).

2. In a small bowl, combine yogurt and baking soda. Set aside.

3. In a large bowl, beat together brown sugar, oil and eggs. Stir in the bran and vanilla.

4. In a third bowl, combine flour, baking powder and salt. Add dry ingredients to sugar mixture alternately with yogurt mixture until thoroughly combined.

5. Gently fold in blueberries.

6. Fill 18 greased large muffin cups and bake for 15 to 20 minutes, or until a toothpick inserted into the centre of a muffin comes out clean.

Makes 18 large muffins

Fresh Orange Muffins

A breakfast muffin that tastes like it has a marmalade filling.

To test cakes and muffins for doneness, stick a wooden skewer or toothpick into the centre of the cake. If the skewer comes out clean, the cake is done.

2	oranges, washed and cut into eighths	2
1 cup	brown sugar	250 mL
2	eggs	2
1/2 cup	vegetable oil	125 mL
1/2 cup	milk	125 mL
1/2 tsp	salt	2 mL
1 tsp	baking soda	5 mL
1 tsp	baking powder	5 mL
1 cup	all-purpose flour	250 mL
1 cup	whole wheat flour	250 mL
1 cup	bran	250 mL
1/2 cup	raisins or chopped walnuts	125 mL

1. Preheat oven to 375° F (190° C).

2. In a food processor, whirl unpeeled oranges with the brown sugar until pureed. Add eggs, oil and milk and blend briefly. Pour into large bowl and set aside.

3. In another bowl, combine salt, baking soda, baking powder, flours and bran.

4. Add dry ingredients to wet ingredients and combine gently until dry ingredients are thoroughly moistened.

5. Stir in raisins or walnuts.

6. Turn batter into 12 greased large muffin cups, and bake for 20 to 25 minutes, or until a toothpick inserted in the centre of a muffin comes out clean.

Makes 12 large muffins

Carrot Muffins

A rich, moist muffin.

1 cup	all-purpose flour	250 mL
1 cup	oat bran	250 mL
2 tsp	baking soda	10 mL
1 tsp	baking powder	5 mL
1/2 tsp	salt	2 mL
2 tsp	cinnamon	10 mL
3/4 cup	brown sugar	175 mL
1-1/2 cups	finely grated carrots	375 mL
2	large tart apples, peeled, cored and grated	2
1/2 cup	raisins	125 mL
1 cup	chopped pecans	250 mL
1/4 cup	vegetable oil	50 mL
1/2 cup	milk	125 mL
2	eggs, lightly beaten	2
1 tsp	vanilla	5 mL

Oat bran is high in fibre. It can be used to replace half the flour in many recipes, because it is an excellent thickener. Try thickening soups, stews and meat loaves with it, too. When used in muffins, oat bran should be combined with other flours, because it contains no gluten and on its own will make baked goods heavy and dense.

1. Preheat oven to 375° F (190° C).

2. In a large bowl, combine all dry ingredients, carrots, apples, raisins and nuts.

3. Make a well in centre of mixture and add oil, milk, eggs and vanilla. Stir until moistened.

4. Fill 12 greased medium muffin cups and bake for 18 to 20 minutes, or until a toothpick inserted in the centre of a muffin comes out clean.

Makes 12 medium muffins

Rocky Mountain Muffins

An excellent healthy muffin with plenty of flavour.

Buttermilk is made from low-fat milk and has only a trace of fat. It is smooth and tangy and adds a refreshing flavour.

1/2 cup	vegetable oil	125 mL
1/2 cup	brown sugar	125 mL
1	egg	1
2 tbsp	molasses	25 mL
1 cup	buttermilk	250 mL
1-1/2 cups	all-purpose flour	375 mL
1/2 cup	whole wheat flour	125 mL
1/2 cup	wheat germ	125 mL
1/4 cup	sunflower seeds	50 mL
1 tsp	baking soda	5 mL
1/2 tsp	salt	2 mL
1/4 tsp	cinnamon	1 mL
1/4 tsp	nutmeg	1 mL
pinch	ground cloves	pinch
1-1/2 cups	raisins	375 mL

1. Preheat oven to 375° F (190° C).

2. In a bowl, beat oil, sugar, egg, molasses and buttermilk together well.

3. In a large bowl, combine remaining ingredients.

4. Add wet ingredients to the dry and stir until just moistened. Pour batter into 16 greased medium muffin cups.

5. Bake for 15 to 20 minutes, or until a toothpick inserted in the centre of a muffin comes out clean.

Makes 16 medium muffins

Oat and Honey Bran Muffins

1 cup	rolled oats	250 mL
3/4 cup	wheat germ	175 mL
1/2 cup	bran	125 mL
1/2 tsp	salt	2 mL
1/2 tsp	cinnamon	2 mL
1 cup	buttermilk or sour milk	250 mL
3/4 cup	honey	175 mL
2	eggs, beaten	2
1/2 cup	vegetable oil	125 mL
1 cup	all-purpose flour	250 mL
2 tsp	baking powder	10 mL
1 tsp	baking soda	5 mL
1 cup	raisins	125 mL

1. Preheat oven to 375° F (190° C).

2. In a large bowl, combine oats, wheat germ, bran, salt, cinnamon and buttermilk. Mix well and let stand for 15 minutes.

3. Beat in honey, eggs and oil.

4. In a separate bowl, combine flour, baking powder and baking soda. Stir into egg mixture. Stir in raisins.

5. Fill 18 greased medium muffin cups.

6. Bake for 20 to 25 minutes, or until a toothpick inserted in the centre of a muffin comes out clean.

Makes 18 medium muffins

Baking soda and baking powder both leaven mixtures, but baking soda must be combined with an acid to give off carbon dioxide, which expands and makes batter rise. Baking powder is a combination of baking soda and an acid; it has a two-part action – one begins working on contact with wet ingredients, and the other works only in the heat of an oven. Baking powder will go stale over time. To test it for freshness, add 1 tsp (5 mL) baking powder to 1/3 cup (75 mL) water. If the baking powder is fresh, the water should rapidly fizzle and bubble.

Pumpkin Blueberry Muffins

Chopped dates, raisins, nuts or chocolate chips can also be used in this recipe from the Ontario Crafts Council, Northern Region.

If you mix your muffin batter too long, or if you do not put the muffins in the oven immediately, the result will be heavy muffins.

4	eggs, beaten	4
2 cups	granulated sugar	500 mL
1-1/2 cups	vegetable oil	375 mL
1-3/4 cups	canned pumpkin	425 mL
3 cups	all-purpose flour	750 mL
1/3 cup	rolled oats	75 mL
1/3 cup	bran	75 mL
2 tsp	baking powder	10 mL
2 tsp	baking soda	10 mL
1 tsp	salt	5 mL
1 tbsp	cinnamon	15 mL
1-1/2 cups	frozen or fresh blueberries	375 mL
2 tbsp	brown sugar	25 mL

1. Preheat oven to 375° F (190° C).

2. In a large bowl, beat eggs, granulated sugar, oil and pumpkin.

3. In a separate bowl, stir together flour, oats, bran, baking powder, baking soda, salt and cinnamon.

4. Add dry ingredients to wet ingredients. Stir until blended.

5. Stir in blueberries.

6. Fill 24 greased medium muffin cups and sprinkle with brown sugar.

7. Bake for 20 minutes, or until a toothpick inserted in the centre of a muffin comes out clean.

Makes 24 medium muffins

Corn Muffins

1-1/2 cups	yellow cornmeal	375 mL
1 cup	all-purpose flour	250 mL
1/2 tsp	baking powder	2 mL
1 tsp	chili powder	5 mL
1/2 tsp	paprika	2 mL
1 tsp	ground cumin	5 mL
1	14-oz (398 mL) can creamed corn	1
1/4 cup	vegetable oil	50 mL
1/4 cup	milk	50 mL
2	eggs, lightly beaten	2
1 cup	grated old Cheddar cheese	250 mL
2 tbsp	chopped green onions or chives	25 mL

Cornmeal is ground corn kernels; it can be white or yellow, depending on the variety of corn. The more yellow the cornmeal, the more vitamin A it contains. Store cornmeal in an airtight jar in a cupboard.

1. Preheat oven to 400° F (200° C).

2. In a large bowl, combine cornmeal, flour, baking powder, chili powder, paprika and cumin.

3. In another bowl, mix creamed corn, oil, milk and eggs. Add to dry ingredients and combine.

4. Fold in cheese and green onions.

5. Fill 12 greased large muffin cups and bake until golden on top, about 20 minutes.

Makes 12 large muffins

Zucchini Loaf

This loaf freezes very well.

3 cups	all-purpose flour	750 mL
1-1/2 cups	granulated sugar	375 mL
1 cup	brown sugar	250 mL
1 tsp	cinnamon	5 mL
1 tsp	salt	5 mL
1 tsp	baking powder	5 mL
1 tsp	baking soda	5 mL
1 cup	chopped nuts	250 mL
1 cup	raisins or chopped dates	250 mL
3	eggs	3
1 cup	vegetable oil	250 mL
1 cup	milk	250 mL
2 cups	shredded zucchini	500 mL

1. Preheat oven to 350° F (180° C).

2. In a bowl, stir together flour, sugars, cinnamon, salt, baking powder, baking soda, nuts and raisins.

3. In a separate large bowl, mix eggs, oil, milk and zucchini.

4. Add dry ingredients to liquid ingredients and stir until well mixed.

5. Pour into two greased 9 x 5-inch (2 L) loaf pans and bake for 1-1/4 to 1-1/2 hours, or until a toothpick in centre of loaf comes out clean.

Makes 2 loaves

Apricot Pecan Loaf

This is a lovely loaf that freezes beautifully.

1/2 cup	dried apricots	125 mL
2 cups	all-purpose flour	500 mL
1 tsp	baking powder	5 mL
1/2 tsp	baking soda	2 mL
1/2 tsp	salt	2 mL
1	egg	1
1 cup	granulated sugar	250 mL
2 tbsp	butter, melted	25 mL
3/4 cup	orange juice	175 mL
1 tbsp	grated orange rind	15 mL
1/2 cup	finely chopped pecans	125 mL
1/2 cup	raisins	125 mL

Fresh apricots consist of about 2% fibre while dried apricots contain 10 times as much.

1. Cover apricots with hot water and soak for 30 minutes. Drain well, then chop in blender or food processor or cut into very thin strips.

2. Preheat oven to 350° F (180° C).

3. In a bowl, sift together the flour, baking powder, baking soda and salt.

4. In a large bowl, beat together the egg, sugar, melted butter and orange juice.

5. Stir the dry ingredients into the egg mixture.

6. Fold in the apricots, orange rind, pecans and raisins. Pour batter into a greased 9 x 5-inch (2 L) loaf pan.

7. Bake for 60 to 70 minutes, or until a toothpick inserted in centre of loaf comes out clean.

8. Remove from oven and let stand for 15 minutes in pan.

Makes 1 loaf

Cranberry-Orange Loaf

1 cup	unsalted butter, at room temperature	250 mL
3/4 cup	granulated sugar	175 mL
4	eggs	4
1-1/2 cups	cake-and-pastry flour	375 mL
2 tsp	baking powder	10 mL
1/2 tsp	salt	2 mL
1/4 cup	freshly squeezed orange juice	50 mL
1 cup	cranberries, coarsely chopped	250 mL

CRANBERRY GLAZE
Set hot loaf on a wire rack placed in a pan with shallow sides. Place 1/2 cup (125 mL) cranberries, 3 tbsp (45 mL) lemon juice and 1/4 cup (50 mL) granulated sugar in a small saucepan over medium heat. Cook, uncovered, until cranberries are very soft, about 5 to 7 minutes, stirring often. Using the back of a spoon, crush cranberries until smooth. Spread over hot loaf and let loaf cool completely.

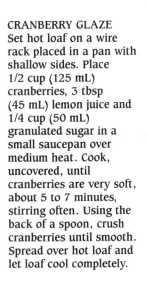

1. Preheat oven to 350° F (180° C).

2. Grease a 9 x 5-inch (2 L) loaf pan and line with waxed paper. Grease waxed paper.

3. In a large bowl of an electric mixer, beat butter with sugar until creamy.

4. Add eggs one at a time, beating well after each addition.

5. In a separate bowl, combine flour, baking powder and salt. Stir with a fork until well blended.

6. Stir flour mixture into creamed mixture alternately with orange juice, ending with flour mixture. Beat after each addition until smooth. Stir in cranberries.

7. Spoon batter into prepared loaf pan and smooth top.

8. Bake for 1 hour and 10 minutes, or until a toothpick inserted in center comes out clean.

9. Remove from oven, set pan on a wire rack and cool for 5 minutes. Turn out of pan and set loaf on wire rack until cooled completely. Wrap and store in the refrigerator or freezer.

Makes 1 loaf

Banana Bread

*Absolutely delicious, easy to make and tastes even better
if kept in a cake tin for a day or two.*

1/2 cup	butter, at room temperature	125 mL
1 cup	granulated sugar	250 mL
1 tsp	vanilla	5 mL
2	eggs	2
2 cups	all-purpose flour	500 mL
2 tsp	baking powder	10 mL
1/2 tsp	salt	2 mL
5	bananas, mashed	5

Three bananas should give you about 1 cup (250 mL) banana purée. Store bananas in the refrigerator; the skin will turn dark, but the flesh should stay pure white.

1. Preheat oven to 350° F (180° C).

2. In a large bowl, cream butter and sugar until light and fluffy. Add vanilla and mix well.

3. Add eggs one at a time, beating well after each addition.

4. In a separate bowl, combine flour, baking powder and salt.

5. Beat dry ingredients into creamed mixture.

6. Mash bananas with a fork and stir into mixture. Mix well.

7. Pour into a greased and floured 9 x 5-inch (2 L) loaf pan.

8. Bake for 1 hour, or until a toothpick inserted in centre of loaf comes out clean.

Makes 1 loaf

Karen Kain's Johnny Cake

Ballet star Karen Kain and her husband, Ross Petty, make this for breakfast. It's also a good quickbread to serve with spicy Caribbean food.

1 cup	granulated sugar	250 mL
1/3 cup	butter, at room temperature	75 mL
1	egg, beaten	1
1 cup	milk	250 mL
1 cup	cornmeal	250 mL
1 cup	all-purpose flour	250 mL
2 tsp	baking powder	10 mL
1/4 tsp	salt	1 mL

1. Preheat oven to 350° F (180° C).

2. In a large bowl, cream together sugar and butter until light and fluffy. Add beaten egg and milk.

3. In a separate bowl, combine cornmeal and flour with baking powder and salt. Stir into creamed mixture.

4. Beat the whole mixture vigorously, then put it in a greased 8-inch (2 L) square baking dish.

5. Bake for 25 minutes, or until a toothpick inserted in centre of cake comes out clean. Cut into squares. Serve hot with butter and maple syrup.

Makes one 8-inch (20 cm) cake

7
Desserts & Pastries

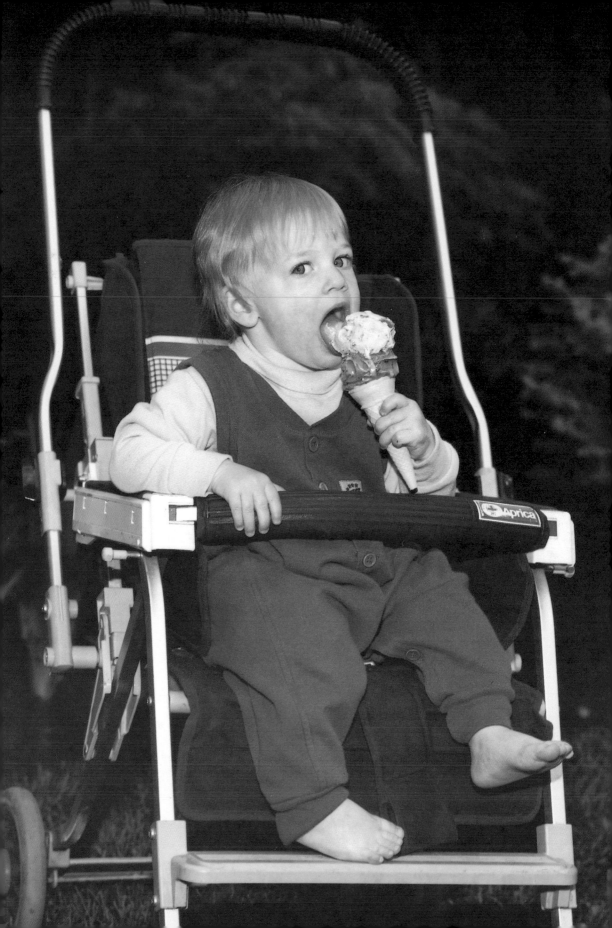

Impossible Pie

This pie is so impossibly good, it gave its name to the book. The recipe comes from former premier of Ontario William Davis's aunt, Winnifred Prouse, who always made this on his birthday.

	Juice and grated rind of 2 lemons	
3	eggs, separated	3
2 tbsp	hot water	25 mL
1/2 cup	granulated sugar	125 mL
2 tbsp	butter	25 mL
1	baked 9-inch (23 cm) pie crust	1

To extract more juice from lemons, limes and oranges, place them in the microwave on high for 30-45 seconds per piece of fruit, or roll them on the kitchen counter with the palms of your hands.

1. In a heavy saucepan, combine lemon juice and rind, egg yolks, hot water, 1/4 cup (50 mL) cup sugar and butter. Heat slowly, stirring constantly, until thick enough to coat a spoon. Remove from heat and allow to cool slightly.

2. In a large bowl, beat egg whites until stiff, slowly adding remaining 1/4 cup (50 mL) sugar. Fold in egg yolk mixture and pour into pie shell.

3. Place pie briefly under broiler to give a golden top. Watch it constantly because it will brown quickly.

Serves 6 to 8

Lovely Pudding

This is a wonderful last-minute dessert.
It is delicious served warm with ice cream.

Pudding

1	egg	1
1/2 cup	granulated sugar	125 mL
1 cup	all-purpose flour	250 mL
1 tsp	baking powder	5 mL
1 tsp	baking soda	5 mL
1-1/2 tsp	white vinegar	7 mL
pinch	salt	pinch
1 tbsp	apricot jam	15 mL
1 cup	milk	250 mL

Syrup

1 cup	granulated sugar	250 mL
1 cup	milk	250 mL
1/4 cup	butter	50 mL
1 tsp	vanilla	5 mL

BUTTERSCOTCH SAUCE
Use this sauce on ice cream, or anything of your choice!
    In a saucepan, combine 1-1/2 cups (375 mL) brown sugar, 1/2 cup (125 mL) corn syrup and 1/4 cup (50 mL) butter. Bring to a boil and cook for 2 to 3 minutes, or until a drop of the mixture forms a soft ball when dropped into cold water. Remove from the heat and cool slightly. Stir in 1/2 cup (125 mL) whipping cream and 1 tsp (5 mL) vanilla. Makes about 2-1/2 cups (625 mL).

1. Preheat oven to 350° F (180° C).

2. In a large bowl, beat the egg and sugar together until soft and fluffy.

3. Add the flour, baking powder, baking soda, vinegar, salt and apricot jam and mix well.

4. Stir in the milk. When well mixed, pour into a greased 8-inch (2 L) square baking dish and bake for 45 minutes, or until a toothpick inserted in centre of pudding comes out clean.

5. In a small saucepan, combine all syrup ingredients. Heat over medium heat until sugar is dissolved. Pour over dessert. Cut into squares.

Serves 8

Old-Fashioned Bread Pudding

This is a spicy cross between a cake and a pudding – perfect for using leftover bread. Try a combination of dried fruit and raisins for a flavour change. The pudding is delicious served hot with custard, but can also be eaten cold.

To prevent milk from burning on the bottom of the pan, rinse the pan out first with water before you pour the milk in.

8 oz	brown or white bread, crusts removed	250 g
1 cup	milk	250 mL
1/4 cup	butter, melted	50 mL
1/2 cup	brown sugar	125 mL
1/4 tsp	cinnamon	1 mL
1/4 tsp	ground ginger	1 mL
1/4 tsp	nutmeg	1 mL
1/4 tsp	ground cloves	1 mL
1	egg, beaten	1
1 cup	raisins or currants	250 mL
	Grated rind of 1 orange	
	Grated nutmeg	

1. Preheat oven to 350° F (180° C).

2. Break bread into pieces and place in a large bowl. Add milk, stir well and let stand for 30 minutes, so that the bread absorbs milk.

3. In a separate bowl, combine melted butter, sugar, spices and beaten egg. Stir in raisins and orange rind. Stir into bread mixture.

4. Spread mixture in a buttered 8-inch (2 L) square baking dish and sprinkle with nutmeg. Bake for 1-1/4 hours, until firm to the touch and golden-brown.

Serves 6

Frozen Strawberry Whip

Delicious and light, very refreshing. Other fresh fruits or frozen juice concentrates (orange juice is particularly good) can be used in place of the strawberries.

2 cups	fresh strawberries	500 mL
2	egg whites	2
1 tbsp	granulated sugar	15 mL

1. Mash the strawberries.

2. In a large bowl, beat egg whites until soft peaks form. Add sugar gradually and beat until stiff peaks form.

3. Gently fold in mashed strawberries, cover and freeze for 2 hours or overnight. Remove dessert from the freezer 20 minutes before serving.

Serves 6

FRUIT FANTASY
Place a variety of fruits in large bowl — watermelon and cantaloupe balls, pineapple chunks, strawberries, mandarin orange segments, apple sections and banana slices. (Dip the apples and bananas in lemon juice first, to prevent browning.)

In a small bowl, combine 2 cups (500 mL) sour cream with 1 tbsp (15 mL) brown sugar and 1 tsp (5 mL) cinnamon. Drizzle the sauce over the fruit before serving.

Mary McGrath's Best Ever Rhubarb Crisp

From Toronto Star *columnist Mary McGrath –*
a quick, easy and delicious crisp. Serve with good-quality
vanilla ice cream, whipped cream or yogurt.

4 cups	chopped rhubarb	1 L
3/4 cup	granulated sugar	175 mL
1/4 cup	all-purpose flour	50 mL
1/2 tsp	cinnamon	2 mL

Topping

1 cup	all-purpose flour	250 mL
3/4 cup	brown sugar	175 mL
1/2 cup	rolled oats	125 mL
1/2 cup	butter, melted	125 mL

1. Preheat oven to 375° F (190° C).

2. In a large bowl, combine rhubarb, granulated sugar, 1/4 cup (50 mL) flour and cinnamon. Place in lightly greased 8-inch (2 L) square baking pan.

3. In a separate bowl, combine topping ingredients. Sprinkle over the rhubarb mixture.

4. Bake for 35 minutes, or until golden brown. Serve hot.

Serves 4 to 6

Ice Cream Pie with Peanut Butter Crust and Fudge Sauce

This pie takes time, but it is dreamy! It can be made early in the day or up to two weeks ahead.

To soften ice cream quickly, place 4 cups (1 L) ice cream in the microwave for 23 seconds at High (100%). For 2 cups (500 mL) ice cream, reduce the time to 14 seconds.

4 cups	vanilla ice cream	1 L
2-1/4 cups	rice cereal	300 mL
1/2 cup	peanut butter	125 mL
1/2 cup	corn syrup	125 mL

Fudge Sauce

3/4 cup	granulated sugar	175 mL
1/2 cup	cocoa	125 mL
1/2 cup	whipping cream	125 mL
1/4 cup	butter	50 mL
1 tsp	vanilla	5 mL

1. Soften 2 cups (500 mL) vanilla ice cream in refrigerator for about 1 hour.

2. Meanwhile, preheat oven to 350° F (180° C). Spread cereal on baking sheet and bake for 5 minutes.

3. In a large bowl, combine peanut butter and corn syrup until blended. Add toasted rice cereal, stirring until well coated. Press cereal mixture evenly into bottom and up sides of a 9-inch (1 L) pie plate.

4. Spread half of softened ice cream over crust. Freeze for 1 hour until firm. Meanwhile, soften remaining ice cream.

5. To prepare fudge sauce, cook sugar, cocoa, whipping cream and butter in a saucepan over medium heat until smooth and boiling, stirring constantly. Remove saucepan from heat and stir in the vanilla. Cool slightly.

6. Pour 1-1/4 cups (300 mL) fudge sauce over ice cream in pie plate and return to freezer again until sauce hardens (about 20 minutes).

7. Put remaining softened ice cream on top of layer of fudge in pie plate. Drizzle remaining fudge in a design on top. Freeze for 3 hours. Wrap in plastic wrap or foil if not serving on same day and return to freezer. Let pie stand at room temperature for 15 minutes before serving.

Serves 12

Frozen Fruit Ice Cream

This is a wonderful topping for waffles, and makes a fantastic dessert or after-school treat.

3	very ripe bananas or peaches	3
4 cups	strawberries	1 L
1/2 cup	milk or orange juice	125 mL
2 tbsp	granulated sugar	25 mL
2 tbsp	lemon juice	25 mL

1. Peel bananas or peaches and cut each into three pieces. Place in freezer bag with strawberries and freeze.

2. When frozen, place fruit in food processor fitted with steel blade. Add just enough milk or juice to aid in blending. Add sugar and lemon juice. Blend until fruit is creamed. Do not overblend. Serve in parfait cups.

Serves 4

To peel peaches: place them in a bowl and cover with boiling water. After 15 seconds remove one to see if the skin comes off easily. If not, put back for a little longer.

Lemon Ice Cream

A frequently requested recipe for a smooth ''no-stir'' ice cream.
It keeps well frozen for several weeks.

Folding: a method of combining a whisked or cream mixture with other ingredients so it remains light. The mixture must be folded very lightly by using a large spoon or spatula.

2	eggs, separated	2
3/4 cup	granulated sugar	175 mL
1/3 cup	lemon juice	75 mL
1 tbsp	grated lemon rind	15 mL
pinch	salt	pinch
1 cup	whipping cream	250 mL

1. In a bowl, beat egg whites until fluffy.

2. Gradually add 1/2 cup (125 mL) sugar and beat whites until stiff. Set aside.

3. In a large bowl, beat yolks with lemon juice, lemon rind and salt.

4. In a separate bowl, combine cream with remaining 1/4 cup (50 mL) sugar. Beat until stiff.

5. Gently fold whipped cream into egg yolk mixture. Fold in egg whites.

6. Cover with foil and freeze overnight. Remove from freezer 20 minutes before serving.

Serves 6 to 8

Hilary Weston's Lemon Pudding

Hilary Weston's favourite pudding cooks with a creamy base and soft crust top. Serve warm or cool with fresh fruit and whipped cream or crème fraîche.

3/4 cup	granulated sugar	175 mL
3 tbsp	all-purpose flour	45 mL
2 tbsp	butter, at room temperature	25 mL
4	eggs, separated	4
1-1/3 cups	milk	325 mL
	Juice and grated rind of 1 lemon	

1. Preheat oven to 325° F (160° C).

2. In a large bowl, combine sugar and flour with an electric mixer. Add soft butter and cream together. Add egg yolks and beat into the mixture until light and fluffy. Add milk, lemon juice and rind and mix thoroughly.

3. In a separate bowl, beat egg whites until stiff but not dry. Lightly fold egg whites into lemon mixture.

4. Pour into a buttered 9-inch (2.5 L) square baking dish. Place a larger pan of hot water in oven and bring to a simmer. Place baking dish in larger pan. Water should come halfway up sides of dish. Bake for 45 to 50 minutes, until a knife inserted in the pudding comes out clean.

Serves 6

There are several easy ways to separate eggs. The easiest method is to break the egg into the palm of your hand and let the white run through your slightly open fingers. If you get some yolk in your whites, remove it with a piece of eggshell.

Myra Sable's Raisin Cinnamon Rice Pudding

1/2 cup	short-grain rice	125 mL
4 cups	milk	1 L
1/4 cup	granulated sugar	50 mL
2 tbsp	butter	25 mL
1/2 tsp	salt	2 mL
1/2 cup	raisins	125 mL
	Cinnamon	
	Granulated sugar	

1. In a saucepan, boil rice in salted boiling water for 10 minutes. Drain well.

2. In a large heavy saucepan, combine rice, milk, sugar, butter and salt. Simmer, uncovered, on low heat, stirring occasionally, for about 40 minutes, or until milk is absorbed. Stir in raisins.

3. Transfer to a bowl. Sprinkle with cinnamon and sugar. Cool and refrigerate until ready to serve.

Serves 4 to 6

Lucy Waverman's Baked Fudge Pudding

This dessert is half a brownie and half steamed pudding.
Serve it warm or cold with whipped cream.

2 cups	granulated sugar	500 mL
1/2 cup	all-purpose flour	125 mL
1/2 cup	cocoa	125 mL
4	eggs, beaten	4
1 cup	butter, melted	250 mL
1 tsp	vanilla	5 mL
1 cup	chopped almonds	250 mL

1. Preheat oven to 325° F (160° C).

2. In a bowl, mix together sugar, flour and cocoa. Stir in eggs, melted butter, vanilla and nuts.

3. Pour batter into a buttered 9-inch (2.5 L) square baking dish. Place larger pan of hot water in oven and allow it to simmer. Place baking dish in larger pan. Water should come halfway up the sides of the dish.

4. Bake for 1 hour and 20 minutes. The pudding is done when the surface is lightly cracked and the centre springs back when touched. The pudding has a custard consistency which firms as it cools. Serve warm or cold in squares.

Serves 8

When a recipe calls for food to be cooked in a *bain marie,* or water bath, it means oven-poaching. To oven-poach, half fill a roasting pan with hot water and place in the oven. When the water simmers, gently place the dish to be cooked in the simmering water. This creates steam in the oven and gently cooks delicate foods such as crème caramel, pâtés, baked puddings or some fish dishes.

Apple Almond Pudding

*The nutty apple flavour and light texture of this pudding
make it perfect for a fall dinner.*

5	tart apples	5
2 cups	fresh breadcrumbs	500 mL
1/3 cup	butter, at room temperature	75 mL
3/4 cup	ground almonds	175 mL
1/2 cup	granulated sugar	125 mL
1	egg	1
1/4 cup	chopped almonds	50 mL

1. Preheat the oven to 350° F (180° C).

2. Peel, core and thinly slice apples. Place in a saucepan, cover and gently stew over low heat until softened. Combine with breadcrumbs.

3. In a bowl, cream together butter, almonds and sugar until light and fluffy. Beat in egg.

4. Place apple/breadcrumb mixture in a greased 9-inch (1 L) pie plate and spread batter over the top. Sprinkle with chopped almonds.

5. Bake for 45 minutes, or until the top is light brown. Serve with whipped cream or ice cream.

Serves 6

Sharon, Lois and Bram's French Toast

For Sharon, Lois and Bram, the most important meal of the day – and the most delicious – is breakfast. They never miss it! Lois uses croissants in this recipe, and serves them with sour cream and fresh berries. Sharon makes hers with challah (egg bread) topped with cottage cheese and strawberry jam. Bram's is on challah, too, topped with Scotch marmalade.

2	eggs, slightly beaten	2
1/2 cup	milk (or a combination of milk and orange juice)	125 mL
1/4 tsp	salt	1 mL
1/4 tsp	vanilla	1 mL
	Grated rind of 1 orange (optional)	
4	slices egg bread, or 2 croissants, split	4
2 tbsp	butter	25 mL

1. In a shallow bowl, combine eggs, milk, salt, vanilla and orange rind. Dip bread into the mixture.

2. In a large skillet, heat butter on medium heat. Sauté bread until golden brown on both sides. Serve immediately.

Makes 4 to 6 slices

Veronica Tennant's Strawberry Meringues

These meringues are a specialty of Veronica Tennant, who learned to make them from her mother, Doris. Veronica won the "Silver Skillet First Prize" at the 1987 Ontario March of Dimes Celebrity Gourmet Gala with this superb recipe.

4	egg whites	4
1/2 tsp	cream of tartar	2 mL
pinch	salt	pinch
1 cup	granulated sugar	250 mL
2 tsp	orange or almond liqueur	10 mL
1 cup	whipping cream	250 mL
2 cups	strawberries, sliced	500 mL

1. Preheat oven to 275° F (140° C).

2. With an electric mixer on high, beat egg whites until frothy. Beat in cream of tartar and salt. Beat again until stiff peaks form on the beater.

3. Gradually beat in sugar 2 tbsp (25 mL) at a time. The mixture will become firm and glossy. Beat in 1 tsp (5 mL) liqueur.

4. Cover a baking sheet with parchment paper. Drop meringue mixture onto the parchment paper by the teaspoonful.

5. Bake for 50 to 60 minutes, or until meringues are dry and do not stick to the parchment paper.

6. At serving time, beat whipping cream until it holds its shape. Beat in remaining liqueur.

7. Place a dollop of whipping cream on a meringue base and top with a second meringue and more cream. Decorate with the strawberries.

Serves 8

Barbara Bush's Orange and Apple Crisp

An easy dessert that the U.S. First Lady serves to her family.

4 cups	sliced, peeled tart apples	1 L
1/4 cup	orange juice	50 mL
1 cup	granulated sugar	250 mL
3/4 cup	all-purpose flour	175 mL
1/2 tsp	cinnamon	2 mL
1/4 tsp	nutmeg	1 mL
pinch	salt	pinch
1/3 cup	butter	75 mL
	Cream	

Adding skim milk powder to any crumb topping is an easy way to add extra protein, calcium and flavour.

1. Preheat oven to 375° F (190° C).

2. Mound apples in a buttered 9-inch (1 L) pie plate. Pour orange juice over the apples.

3. In a bowl, combine sugar, flour, cinnamon, nutmeg and salt. Cut in butter until mixture is crumbly. Sprinkle over apples.

4. Bake for 45 minutes, or until the apples are tender and the topping is crisp. Serve warm with cream.

Serves 4

Butter Tarts

The best butter tarts ever! If you don't have maple syrup, use corn syrup instead.

1 cup	brown sugar	250 mL
1/4 cup	butter, at room temperature	50 mL
1/2 cup	maple syrup	125 mL
2	eggs, beaten	2
1 tbsp	white vinegar	15 mL
1/2 cup	chopped walnuts (optional)	125 mL
1/2 cup	raisins	125 mL
12	unbaked 3-inch (7.5 cm) tart shells	12

1. Preheat oven to 375° F (190° C).

2. In a bowl, beat together sugar, butter, maple syrup, eggs and vinegar.

3. Divide walnuts and raisins among tart shells. Pour syrup mixture over to fill shells three-quarters full.

4. Bake for 25 minutes, or until mixture bubbles and tart shells are golden.

Makes 12 tarts

Joyce Trimmer's Trifle

The mayor of Scarborough calls this her "tried and true trifle."
In the British tradition, Joyce uses Bird's custard, a great custard
powder that makes a creamy mixture and tastes homemade.

1	8-inch (20 cm) sponge cake	1
1/2 cup	raspberry jam	125 mL
1/3 cup	sherry	75 mL
2 cups	frozen raspberries, defrosted	500 mL
2-1/2 cups	milk	625 mL
3 tbsp	custard powder	45 mL
2 tbsp	granulated sugar	25 mL
1 cup	whipping cream	250 mL
2 tbsp	Drambuie	25 mL

1. Split sponge cake in half horizontally. Spread both halves with jam and cut into large chunks.

2. Place cake, jam side up, in a bowl or serving dish. Pour sherry over and sprinkle on raspberries.

3. In a small bowl, blend 1/3 cup (75 mL) milk with custard powder and sugar.

4. Bring the remaining milk to boil in saucepan. Slowly pour hot milk into the custard mixture, stirring. Return to saucepan.

5. Return the saucepan to heat and bring to a boil, stirring until thickened. Place plastic wrap on top of the custard to prevent a skin from forming. When custard has cooled, spread it over sponge cake mixture.

6. In a large bowl, whip the cream until thickened. Whisk in the Drambuie. Spread cream over trifle.

Serves 6 to 8

Deep-Dish Rhubarb Grunt

*This recipe is easy to whip up. It has a scone-like topping
that is very popular in eastern Canada.*

When buying rhubarb,
look for deep-pink stalks,
which are sweeter than
green. Hot house
rhubarb is usually
sweeter than the garden
variety; if you are using
sweet rhubarb, reduce
the amount of sugar
in the recipe.

Filling

5 cups	sliced rhubarb	1.25 L
3/4 cup	granulated sugar	175 mL
2 tbsp	water	25 mL

Topping

2 cups	all-purpose flour	500 mL
4 tsp	baking powder	20 mL
2 tbsp	granulated sugar	25 mL
1/2 tsp	salt	2 mL
1/2 cup	butter or shortening	125 mL
1	egg, beaten	1
1 cup	milk	250 mL

1. Preheat oven to 400° F (200° C).

2. In a saucepan, place rhubarb, 3/4 cup (175 mL) sugar and water.
Simmer for 10 minutes, or until rhubarb is tender. Spoon into a greased
9-inch (23 cm) pie plate and cool.

3. In a bowl, combine flour, baking powder, 2 tbsp (25 mL) sugar and
salt. Cut butter into dry mixture until crumbly.

4. In a separate bowl, combine egg and milk. Blend gently into the flour
mixture. Place dough on floured surface. Knead lightly. Cut with 2-inch
(5 cm) cutter and place on cooled rhubarb.

5. Bake for 12 to 15 minutes, or until topping is golden.

Serves 6

Apple Flan

This is a rich recipe for company. It is easy to make and always works.

Base

1 cup	all-purpose flour	250 mL
1/2 cup	granulated sugar	125 mL
1/2 cup	butter	125 mL

Filling

8 oz	cream cheese, at room temperature	250 g
1/4 cup	granulated sugar	50 mL
1	egg	1
1/2 tsp	vanilla	2 mL

Topping

1/4 cup	granulated sugar	50 mL
1/2 tsp	cinnamon	2 mL
1/4 cup	chopped nuts	50 mL
4 cups	sliced apples	1 L

Vanilla is made from the seed pod of a climbing plant related to the orchid family. Whole vanilla pods can be used to flavour milk puddings; the essence, commercially made, can be used in cakes, puddings and cookies.

1. Preheat oven to 450° F (230° C).

2. To prepare base, in a bowl or food processor, blend flour and sugar. Add butter and blend until crumbly. Pat into a 9-inch (23 cm) springform pan. Bake for 10 minutes, remove from oven and reduce oven temperature to 400° F (200° C).

3. To prepare filling, in a bowl, blend the cream cheese, sugar, egg and vanilla. Pour over top of base.

4. To prepare the topping, in a separate bowl, combine sugar, cinnamon and nuts.

5. Layer the apples over the cream cheese filling and sprinkle with the topping mixture.

6. Bake for 25 minutes. Let cool before removing from pan.

Serves 8

Brandy Squares

*This is a South African recipe. It is moist and simply delicious
with cream. To change the flavour of the dessert,
use orange liqueur instead of brandy.*

Creaming: the beating
together of fat and sugar
until it resembles
whipped cream in colour
and texture.

1/2 cup	butter, at room temperature	125 mL
1 cup	granulated sugar	250 mL
2	eggs	2
1-1/2 cups	all-purpose flour	375 mL
1/2 tsp	baking powder	2 mL
1/4 tsp	salt	1 mL
1/2 cup	chopped nuts	125 mL
1 cup	boiling water	250 mL
1 cup	chopped dates	250 mL
1 tsp	baking soda	5 mL

Brandy Syrup

1 cup	granulated sugar	250 mL
1/2 cup	water	125 mL
1 tbsp	butter	15 mL
1/2 tsp	vanilla	2 mL
1/4 cup	brandy	50 mL

1. Preheat oven to 350° F (180° C).

2. In a large bowl, cream butter and sugar until soft and fluffy. Add eggs
and beat well.

3. In a separate bowl, combine flour, baking powder and salt. Stir into
egg mixture. Fold in the nuts.

4. In small bowl, pour boiling water over dates. Add baking soda and
let it bubble. Pour date mixture into batter and mix well.

5. Pour batter into a greased 11 x 9-inch (2˙L) baking dish and bake for 30 to 40 minutes, or until a toothpick inserted in tart comes out clean.

6. Meanwhile, to make syrup, in a saucepan combine sugar, water and butter. Bring to a boil and simmer for 5 minutes, or until syrup is a golden colour.

7. Remove from heat and stir in vanilla and brandy. When bubbles disappear, pour syrup over tart just as it comes out of the oven. Serve cold with whipped cream.

Serves 10

Three-Layer Coconut Pie

An easy pie that miraculously forms a crust with a custard centre and a coconut topping.

2	eggs	2
1/4 cup	butter, at room temperature	50 mL
1/4 cup	all-purpose flour	50 mL
1 cup	milk	250 mL
1/2 cup	granulated sugar	125 mL
1/2 cup	grated coconut	125 mL
1 tbsp	vanilla	15 mL

1. Preheat oven to 350° F (180° C).

2. In a large bowl, mix all ingredients together by hand, blender or food processor. Pour into a greased 10-inch (1.5 L) pie pan.

3. Bake for approximately 1 hour, until toothpick inserted in pie comes out clean. The flour will settle to form a crust, the coconut forms a topping and the centre is an egg custard filling. Serve warm.

Serves 6

Fresh Raspberry Pie

This is the most divine fruit pie you could ever savour! Make this pie until raspberry season is over. After that, substitute any berries for raspberries. Don't use frozen raspberries; they will make the pie watery.

Raspberries are an excellent source of fibre–essential in maintaining a healthy diet.

4 cups	fresh raspberries (or your favourite berry)	1 L
1 cup	granulated sugar	250 mL
3 tbsp	cornstarch	45 mL
1	baked 9-inch (23 cm) pie crust	1

1. In a saucepan, combine 2 cups (500 mL) berries with sugar and cornstarch and stir gently over low heat until mixture is thick and clear. Allow to cool.

2. Spread remaining berries in pie shell. Spread cooked mixture on top of fresh berries. Serve with whipped cream.

Serves 6

Open-Face Peach Pie

If you can, use a deep-dish crust for this pie.

3/4 cup	granulated sugar	175 mL
1/4 cup	all-purpose flour	50 mL
2 tbsp	butter	25 mL
7	fresh peaches, peeled, cored and cut in half	7
1/4 cup	water	50 mL
2 tbsp	lemon juice	25 mL
1/4 tsp	almond extract	1 mL
1	unbaked 9-inch (23 cm) pie crust	1

1. Preheat oven to 375° F (190° C).

2. In a bowl, blend sugar and flour. Cut in butter until mixture resembles coarse crumbs.

3. Sprinkle half of crumb mixture in unbaked crust. Arrange peaches, cut side down, on top. Cover with the rest of the crumbs.

4. In a bowl, combine water, lemon juice and almond extract. Pour over pie.

5. Bake for 40 to 50 minutes, or until juices are bubbling and fruit is tender.

Serves 8

In clingstone peaches, the peach flesh adheres to the pit. These peaches are usually available earlier in the season and are mostly used for canning. In freestone peaches, the flesh does not adhere to the pit. They are the best for eating and pies. The best-known freestone variety is Red Haven.

Schnitz Pie

A traditional Mennonite recipe.

2 tbsp	fresh breadcrumbs	25 mL
1	unbaked 9-inch (23 cm) pie crust	1
5 cups	peeled and sliced cooking apples	1.25 L

Topping

3/4 cup	granulated sugar	175 mL
1-1/4 cups	sour cream	300 mL
3 tbsp	all-purpose flour	45 mL
1	egg	1
1 tsp	vanilla	5 mL
1 tsp	cinnamon	5 mL
1/4 cup	slivered almonds	50 mL

1. Preheat oven to 450° F (230° C).

2. Sprinkle breadcrumbs on bottom of pie shell. Arrange apple slices decoratively on top.

3. In a bowl, combine all topping ingredients except cinnamon and almonds. Pour over apples. Sprinkle cinnamon and almonds over the pie.

4. Bake for 15 minutes. Turn temperature down to 350° F (180° C) and bake for 35 minutes, or until fruit is soft. Serve warm or cool.

Serves 8

8
Cakes

Ice Cream Cake

3 cups	Rice Krispies	750 mL
1/2 cup	chopped nuts	125 mL
1/4 cup	butter	50 mL
6 oz	semi-sweet chocolate	175 g
4 cups	butter pecan or chocolate ice cream, softened	1 L

Topping

1 cup	whipping cream	250 mL
2 tbsp	granulated sugar	25 mL
1 tsp	instant coffee powder	5 mL
2 tbsp	cocoa	25 mL
	Shaved semi-sweet chocolate	

1. In a bowl, combine Rice Krispies and chopped nuts.

2. In a large saucepan on low heat, melt butter and chocolate. Stir in Rice Krispies and nut mixture. Spread this mixture in bottom of a 9-inch (23 cm) springform pan. Spread on softened ice cream and freeze for 15 minutes, or until hard.

3. In a bowl, whip cream and sugar until cream holds its shape. Stir in coffee and cocoa.

4. Spread topping mixture over cake. Sprinkle with shaved chocolate. Freeze until 20 minutes before serving. Unmould and cut into slices.

Serves 8

Fudge Candy Cake

1/2 cup	butter, at room temperature	125 mL
1 cup	granulated sugar	250 mL
2	eggs	2
1/2 cup	all-purpose flour	125 mL
1 cup	chopped walnuts	250 mL
1 tsp	vanilla	5 mL
2 tbsp	cocoa	25 mL
pinch	salt	pinch

Icing

2 tbsp	butter, at room temperature	25 mL
2 tbsp	cocoa	25 mL
3 tbsp	boiling water	45 mL
1 cup	icing sugar	250 mL
1/2 tsp	vanilla	2 mL

When making cakes, always cream the butter and sugar together until the mixture is very light and fluffy, with no grains of sugar visible. This process adds air to the cake. Use an electric mixer if you have one, and allow the butter to soften to room temperature before combining it with the sugar.

1. Preheat oven to 350° F (180° C).

2. In a bowl, cream butter and sugar together until light and fluffy. Add one egg at a time, beating well after each addition. Beat in flour. Stir in walnuts, vanilla, cocoa and salt.

3. Spread batter in a buttered and floured 8-inch (20 cm) cake pan.

4. Bake for 30 minutes, or until a toothpick inserted in the cake comes out clean.

5. In a bowl, combine icing ingredients.

6. Pour icing onto cake as soon as it is taken from the oven. The icing should sink through the cake.

Serves 8

Orange Cake

1-1/2 cups	granulated sugar	375 mL
1/2 cup	butter or shortening, at room temperature	125 mL
2	eggs	2
2 cups	all-purpose flour	500 mL
1 tsp	baking soda	5 mL
	Grated rind and juice of 1 orange	
1 cup	sour milk	250 mL
1 cup	chopped raisins	250 mL
1/2 cup	chopped nuts	125 mL

To make sour milk, combine 1 cup (250 mL) milk with 1 tbsp (15 mL) lemon juice. Let stand for 30 minutes.

1. Preheat oven to 350° F (180° C).

2. In a large bowl, beat together 1 cup (250 mL) sugar and butter until light and fluffy. Add eggs one at a time, beating well after each addition.

3. In a separate bowl, combine flour, baking soda and orange rind.

4. Stir flour mixture into egg mixture alternately with sour milk. Stir in raisins and nuts. Spread batter in a buttered 13 x 9-inch (3.5 L) baking dish.

5. Bake for 30 to 35 minutes, or until a toothpick inserted in the cake comes out clean.

6. In a small bowl, mix together orange juice and remaining 1/2 cup (125 mL) sugar. Pour over cake while still warm.

Serves 8 to 10

Coconut Cake

This family favourite can be put together in just a few minutes.
It bakes in the time it takes to eat your first course.

Coconut is an excellent source of potassium and also contains iron.

1/2 cup	butter, at room temperature	125 mL
1 cup	granulated sugar	250 mL
3	eggs, separated	3
1 cup	all-purpose flour	250 mL
1-1/2 tsp	baking powder	7 mL
1/2 cup	milk	125 mL
1/2 cup	finely grated coconut	125 mL

1. Preheat oven to 350° F (180° C).

2. In a bowl, cream butter and 1/2 cup (125 mL) sugar until light and fluffy. Beat in egg yolks one at a time.

3. In a separate bowl, combine flour and baking powder. Fold into creamed mixture alternately with milk and mix just until smooth.

4. Spread batter in a greased 8-inch (2L) square baking dish.

5. In a bowl, beat egg whites and remaining 1/2 cup (125 mL) sugar until stiff. Fold in coconut. Spread over mixture in the pan.

6. Bake for 20 to 25 minutes, or until nicely brown. Serve hot.

Serves 6 to 8

Chocolate Cake

A wonderfully easy recipe for a deliciously moist cake.

3	squares unsweetened chocolate	3
1-1/2 cups	boiling water	375 mL
4	eggs	4
2 cups	granulated sugar	500 mL
1 cup	vegetable oil	250 mL
2-2/3 cups	all-purpose flour	650 mL
1 tsp	baking powder	5 mL
1 tsp	baking soda	5 mL
1/2 tsp	salt	2 mL
1 tsp	vanilla	5 mL
1/2 cup	icing sugar	125 mL

To melt chocolate in the microwave, use Medium (50%) power and microwave for about 2 minutes per ounce (30 g).

1. Preheat oven to 325° F (160° C).

2. In a small bowl, heat chocolate and boiling water. Stir together until melted. Cool.

3. With an electric mixer, beat eggs in large bowl. Gradually add the granulated sugar and oil. Beat at high speed until well combined, about 2 minutes. Lower speed and beat in the chocolate mixture.

4. In a bowl, combine flour, baking powder, baking soda and salt. On low speed, slowly add dry ingredients to the mixer. Add vanilla.

5. Spread batter in a greased and floured 13 x 9-inch (3.5 L) baking dish. Bake for 45 minutes, or until a toothpick inserted in the cake comes out clean. Cool. Dust cake with icing sugar before serving.

Serves 8 to 10

Mila Mulroney's Mandarin Cheesecake

The Mulroney children love this cheesecake, which is made on special occasions. Garnish the cake with coarsely chopped praline and a few slices of fresh mandarin orange.

PRALINE
In a saucepan, combine 1 lb (500 g) peeled and blanched almonds, 1 cup (250 mL) granulated sugar, 1-1/2 tsp (7 mL) salt and 1/4 cup (50 mL) water. Bring to a boil and cook, stirring, until the water evaporates and the sugar turns a light-gold colour. Spread mixture on a buttered baking sheet and bake at 300° F (150° C) for 25 minutes. When cool, break into pieces.

	Grated rind and juice of 3 mandarin oranges	
	Grated rind and juice of 1 lemon	
2 tbsp	unflavoured gelatin	25 mL
4	eggs, separated	4
1-1/4 cups	milk	300 mL
1 lb	cream cheese, at room temperature	500 g
2/3 cup	granulated sugar	150 mL
1/4 cup	orange liqueur	50 mL
3/4 cup	mandarin or apricot jam	175 mL
1 cup	whipping cream	250 mL
2	packages Italian ladyfingers	2

1. In a small bowl, combine mandarin and lemon juices and rinds. Add gelatin and stir well until thoroughly dissolved.

2. Combine egg yolks and milk in a heavy saucepan. Heat slowly, stirring constantly with a whisk so that egg yolks cook but do not curdle. Remove from heat and add mandarin juice mixture. Stir well with whisk to make sure gelatin is completely dissolved. Set aside to cool.

3. In a large bowl, beat cream cheese with the sugar. Add half of the orange liqueur and beat again. Add the egg/juice mixture and cool, stirring occasionally so that the mixture sets evenly.

4. When mixture has reached the consistency of loose custard, add the jam and mix well so that it is evenly distributed.

5. In a separate bowl, whip cream until stiff. Fold into cheese mixture.

6. In a separate bowl, beat egg whites until stiff but not dry. Add one-third of whites to cheese mixture to lighten it, then gently fold in the remaining egg whites so that they are well combined but retain their volume.

7. Line bottom and sides of a 10-inch (3 L) springform pan with ladyfingers. Sprinkle bottom with remaining liqueur. Pour in cheese mixture and allow to set in the refrigerator for at least 4 hours or overnight.

Serves 12

Gingerbread Sponge Cake

2 cups	self-rising flour	500 mL
1/2 cup	margarine, at room temperature	125 mL
2 tbsp	corn syrup	25 mL
1/2 tsp	baking soda	2 mL
1 cup	granulated sugar	250 mL
1	egg	1
1 to 2 tsp	ground ginger	5 to 10 mL
1 cup	milk	250 mL

SELF-RISING FLOUR
Self-rising flour contains both baking powder and salt. To make your own, combine 2 cups (500 mL) all-purpose flour with 1 tsp (5 mL) baking powder and 1/4 tsp (1 mL) salt.

1. Preheat the oven to 300° F (150° C).

2. In a large mixing bowl, combine all ingredients except milk. Bring milk to boil and pour over mixture. Mix into a thick batter and turn into a greased 8-inch (2 L) square baking dish.

3. Bake for approximately 45 minutes, or until cake springs back when pressed. Cool.

Serves 8

Miniature Cheesecakes

*This excellent tart recipe is easy to make and great
for lunch boxes. Top with fresh fruit, if desired.*

8 to 10	vanilla wafers	8 to 10
8 oz	cream cheese, at room temperature	250 g
1/3 cup	granulated sugar	75 mL
1	egg	1
2 tbsp	lemon juice	25 mL
1/2 tsp	vanilla	2 mL

1. Preheat the oven to 375° F (190° C).

2. Line muffin tins with paper baking cups. Place a vanilla wafer in each cup.

3. In a bowl, beat the remaining ingredients together until light and fluffy. Fill cups two-thirds full with cheese mixture.

4. Bake for 15 to 20 minutes, or until mixture is firm.

Serves 8 to 10

Amaretto Cheesecake

1-1/2 lb	cream cheese, at room temperature	750 g
1 cup	granulated sugar	250 mL
4	eggs	4
1/3 cup	Amaretto	75 mL
1	9-inch (23 cm) Graham cracker crust	1

Topping

1 cup	sour cream	250 mL
2 tbsp	granulated sugar	25 mL
2 tbsp	Amaretto	25 mL
1/2 cup	sliced almonds, toasted	125 mL
	Grated chocolate	
	Strawberry halves	

GRAHAM CRACKER CRUST
Combine 1-1/4 cups (300 mL) Graham cracker crumbs with 1 tsp (5 mL) sugar and 1/4 cup (50 mL) melted butter. Pat into a 9-inch (23 cm) pie plate.

1. Preheat oven to 375° F (190° C).

2. In a mixer, beat cream cheese at high speed until light and fluffy. Gradually add 1 cup (250 mL) sugar, beating well. Add eggs one at a time, beating well after each addition. Stir in 1/3 cup (75 mL) Amaretto.

3. Pour mixture into the prepared crust. Bake for 45 to 50 minutes, or until set. Increase oven heat to 500° F (250° C).

4. In a bowl, combine sour cream, 2 tbsp (25 mL) sugar and 2 tbsp (25 mL) Amaretto. Stir well and spoon over cheesecake.

5. Bake for 5 minutes. Let cool at room temperature on a wire rack. Chill.

6. Garnish cake with sliced almonds, grated chocolate and strawberry halves.

Serves 8 to 10

Old-Fashioned Jelly Roll

1 cup	cake and pastry flour	250 mL
1 tsp	baking powder	5 mL
1/4 tsp	salt	1 mL
4	eggs	4
1/4 cup	water	50 mL
1 tsp	lemon juice	5 mL
1 cup	granulated sugar	250 mL
	Icing sugar	
2 cups	jam, jelly or lemon curd	500 mL

For a perfectly round jelly roll, after the cake has been rolled in the tea towel, tie a long piece of string to each end of the towel. Hang the roll from a doorknob to cool.

1. Preheat oven to 400° F (200° C).

2. Lightly grease a 15 x 10-inch (2 L) jelly roll pan and line with parchment paper.

3. In a bowl, sift together flour, baking powder and salt and set aside.

4. In a large bowl, beat eggs and water until thick. Gradually beat in lemon juice and sugar. Continue to beat until very thick. Fold the dry ingredients into the egg mixture in four additions. Turn into prepared pan.

5. Bake for 10 minutes, or until golden.

6. As soon as cake is removed from the oven, turn out onto a clean tea towel sprinkled with icing sugar. Remove paper and roll up cake in towel, along the long side.

7. When cool, unroll and fill with jam, jelly or lemon filling. Reroll and serve.

Makes 1 jelly roll

Carrot Cake

*We received many recipes for carrot cake, but this was the best!
It is great served as a snack, or after dinner with coffee.*

4	eggs	4
1/2 cup	liquid honey	125 mL
1/2 cup	brown sugar	125 mL
1/2 cup	vegetable oil	125 mL
3 cups	finely grated carrots	750 mL
1 tsp	vanilla	5 mL
2 tsp	cinnamon	10 mL
1/2 tsp	nutmeg	2 mL
2 cups	whole wheat flour	500 mL
2 tsp	baking powder	10 mL
1/2 tsp	baking soda	2 mL
1/2 cup	raisins	125 mL
1/2 cup	chopped walnuts	125 mL
	Icing sugar	

Whole wheat flour is made from the whole grain of wheat. Along with fibre it also contains some fat. Whole wheat flour has a shorter shelf life because of its fat content, so buy it in small quantities. It is more nutritious and contains vitamins of the B group, vitamin E, and minerals.

1. Preheat oven to 350° F (180° C). Grease and flour the bottom and sides of a 9-inch (2.5 L) springform pan.

2. In a large bowl, beat eggs, honey, sugar and oil with a wire whisk until well blended. Stir in carrots, vanilla, cinnamon and nutmeg.

3. In a separate bowl, combine flour, baking powder, baking soda, raisins and walnuts. Stir until thoroughly blended.

4. Pour flour mixture over carrot mixture. With rubber spatula, fold in flour mixture until well blended. Pour batter into the prepared pan.

5. Bake for 55 to 60 minutes, or until a toothpick inserted deep into centre of cake comes out clean. Cool in pan or on rack.

6. Sprinkle top of cooled cake lightly with icing sugar.

Serves 8

Maureen Forrester's Chocolate-Orange Cheesecake

Maureen Forrester enjoyed this cake while on a promotional tour and it is still one of her favourites. She says it's guaranteed to get a standing ovation! Be sure to drizzle the chocolate on the crumb mixture. Spreading it with a knife will disturb the crust and make the cake difficult to cut.

2 cups	digestive biscuit crumbs	500 mL
2 tbsp	butter, melted	25 mL
4 oz	semi-sweet chocolate	125 g
1-1/2 lbs	cream cheese, at room temperature	750 g
1/3 cup	frozen orange juice concentrate, thawed	75 mL
1/2 cup	granulated sugar	125 mL

1. In a bowl, combine biscuit crumbs with butter. Press into a buttered 8-inch (2 L) springform pan.

2. In a saucepan, melt chocolate over low heat. Drizzle chocolate on top of the biscuit mixture. Refrigerate.

3. In a large bowl, beat cream cheese with sugar and orange juice to a smooth consistency. Spread over the hardened chocolate. Chill thoroughly before serving.

Serves 8

9
Cookies
& Candies

Mini Walnut Crescents

3/4 cup	butter, at room temperature	175 mL
1-1/2 cups	granulated sugar	375 mL
1	egg white	1
1 cup	chopped walnuts	250 mL
1 tsp	vanilla	5 mL
1-1/2 cups	all-purpose flour	375 mL

If you have a leftover egg yolk, beat it and cover with plastic wrap. Refrigerate for up to 3 days and use in omelettes, scrambled eggs, Caesar salad dressing, mayonnaise, and for brushing on pastry.

1. Preheat oven to 375° F (190° C).

2. In a large bowl, beat butter and 1/2 cup (125 mL) sugar until creamy and smooth.

3. In a separate bowl, beat egg white until fluffy; add it to the first mixture along with the walnuts and vanilla.

4. Gradually mix in the flour until you can form balls.

5. Shape dough into small crescents, a teaspoonful at a time. Roll the crescents in the remaining 1 cup (250 mL) sugar and place on a greased baking sheet.

6. Bake for 12-15 minutes, or until slightly golden.

Makes about 36 2-inch (5 cm) cookies

Chocolate Cream Cheese Brownies

Pack these brownies in children's lunch boxes,
or serve as an after-school snack.

When baking, always use room temperature eggs if possible. You will get more volume than you would from cold eggs.

6 oz	semi-sweet chocolate	175 g
2 tbsp	butter	25 mL
1/2 cup	all-purpose flour	125 mL
1/2 tsp	baking powder	2 mL
3	eggs	3
1-1/2 tsp	vanilla	7 mL
1 cup	granulated sugar	250 mL
1 tbsp	lemon juice	15 mL
4 oz	cream cheese, at room temperature	125 g

1. Preheat oven to 350° F (180° C).

2. In a saucepan, melt chocolate and butter. Set aside to cool.

3. In a bowl, stir together flour and baking powder.

4. In a large bowl, beat 2 eggs, vanilla and sugar until light and fluffy. Add dry ingredients and beat well. Stir in chocolate and butter.

5. In a separate bowl, beat remaining egg, lemon juice and cream cheese.

6. Alternately pour chocolate mixture and cream cheese mixture into a greased and lightly floured 8-inch (2 L) square baking pan. Swirl layers to marble.

7. Bake for 45 minutes. Allow to cool. Cut up into bars.

Makes 24 bars

Banana Granola Bars

*Bake these bars in paper muffin cups, so they can
be carried easily in school lunch boxes.
The baked bars can also be frozen.*

1/2 cup	butter	125 mL
1/4 cup	maple or corn syrup	50 mL
2 tbsp	brown sugar	25 mL
2 cups	rolled oats	500 mL
1/2 cup	raisins	125 mL
1	small banana, mashed	1

1. Preheat oven to 350° F (180° C).

2. In a saucepan, heat butter, syrup and sugar until evenly blended. Stir in the oats, raisins and mashed banana.

3. Line a muffin pan with 12 paper cups. Divide mixture among cups.

4. Bake for 25 to 30 minutes, or until firm to the touch. Leave to cool. Store in airtight container for up to a week.

Makes 12 bars

**Cookies should be
completely cooled before
being stored in
airtight containers.**

Mary McGrath's Whipped Shortbread Cookies

Mary McGrath, the Toronto Star's *home economist, got this recipe from Sigrid McFarland, and she has been making these cookies ever since, especially throughout the Christmas season. Chocolate chunks or chips can be substituted for the pecans.*

Grease baking sheets with oil or use parchment paper, a non-stick baking paper that can be bought at supermarkets. Buttered baking sheets will burn at a lower temperature than oiled ones.

2 cups	butter, at room temperature	500 mL
1 cup	icing sugar	250 mL
1/2 cup	cornstarch	125 mL
1 tsp	vanilla	5 mL
3 cups	all-purpose flour	750 mL
1 cup	chopped pecans	250 mL

1. Preheat oven to 325° F (160° C).

2. In a large bowl, cream butter and icing sugar until very fluffy. Beat in cornstarch and vanilla. Beat in flour until batter is light and very fluffy. Stir in nuts.

3. Drop batter by the teaspoonful 1-1/2 inches (4 cm) apart on lightly greased baking sheets. Bake for 20 to 25 minutes, or until golden.

4. Dust lightly with sifted icing sugar before serving, if desired.

Makes about 60 cookies

Lace Cookies

*An easy recipe for those delectable lacy cookies
that melt in your mouth.*

2 cups	brown sugar	500 mL
2-1/4 cups	rolled oats	50 mL
1/2 tsp	salt	2 mL
1 cup	butter, melted	250 mL
1	egg	1
1/2 tsp	vanilla	2 mL
1 tbsp	all-purpose flour	15 mL

1. Preheat oven to 350° F (180 C°).

2. In a bowl, combine sugar, oats and salt.

3. In a separate bowl, combine butter, egg, vanilla and flour. Combine second mixture with first. It will be a soft mixture.

4. Chill dough for 30 minutes. Drop small spoonfuls on lightly oiled baking sheets, leaving a 3-inch (7.5 cm) space between the cookies.

5. Bake for 5 to 7 minutes, or until pale gold.

Makes about 36 cookies

Lace cookies can be served with ice cream or any custard-like dessert. To make them even richer, spread the underside with melted chocolate.

Poppy Seed Cookies

For a flavour variation, add the grated rind of one orange to the batter.

1 cup	granulated sugar	250 mL
1/2 cup	poppy seeds	125 mL
3 cups	all-purpose flour	750 mL
2 tsp	baking powder	10 mL
1/2 tsp	salt	2 mL
1 cup	butter	250 mL
1 tsp	vanilla	5 mL
2	eggs	2

1. Preheat oven to 350° F (180° C).

2. In a large bowl, combine sugar, poppy seeds, flour, baking powder and salt. Cut in butter until mixture is crumbly.

3. In a separate bowl, combine vanilla and eggs. Stir into butter mixture.

4. Roll out dough until 1/4 inch (5 mm) thick. Cut into 2-inch (5 cm) rounds.

5. Place on baking sheet and bake for 15 minutes, or until pale gold.

Makes about 36 cookies

Praline Squares

Absolutely delicious! Easy to make, and they freeze beautifully.

30	Graham crackers (approx.)	30
1 cup	butter	250 mL
1 cup	brown sugar	250 mL
2 cups	sliced almonds	500 mL
2 tbsp	sesame seeds	25 mL

Sesame seeds are high in fibre and a source of iron. They make a great snack for children. To toast in the microwave, place 1/4 cup of sesame seeds in a bowl, cook at high for 2-1/2 to 3-1/2 minutes, stirring twice.

1. Preheat oven to 375° F (190° C).

2. Line a rimmed baking sheet with foil, shiny side down. Cover entire surface with Graham crackers.

3. In a saucepan, bring butter, sugar, almonds and sesame seeds to a boil. Boil for 3 minutes. Pour over crackers.

4. Bake for 8 minutes, or until mixture is bubbly. Let cool for 5 minutes before cutting into rectangles.

Makes about 60 squares

Lime Sugar Cookies

A delightful aromatic cookie. Use fresh lime juice for the best results.

Bake cookies on the middle rack of the oven for even baking. If you use the two racks at the same time, change the position of the baking sheets halfway through the baking time.

1/2 cup	butter, at room temperature	125 mL
1/2 cup	granulated sugar	125 mL
pinch	salt	pinch
	Juice and grated rind of 1 lime	
1-1/2 cups	all-purpose flour	375 mL
1 tsp	granulated sugar	5 mL

1. In a bowl, cream butter and 1/2 cup (125 mL) sugar with an electric mixer. Beat in salt and lime juice. Stir in flour with a wooden spoon. Chill for at least 1 hour.

2. Preheat the oven to 375° F (190° C).

3. Shape dough into two rolls, 4 inches (10 cm) long. Cut rolls into 1/4-inch (5 mm) slices and place on ungreased baking sheet 1 inch (2.5 cm) apart.

4. In a small bowl, combine 1 tsp (5 mL) sugar and lime rind. Sprinkle on cookies.

5. Bake for 6 to 8 minutes, or until bottoms of cookies are golden.

Makes about 60 cookies

Newfoundland's Best Ever Drop Cookies

2 cups	all-purpose flour	500 mL
1/2 tsp	baking powder	2 mL
1/2 tsp	baking soda	2 mL
1/2 tsp	salt	2 mL
1 tsp	cinnamon	5 mL
1/2 tsp	nutmeg	2 mL
3/4 cup	butter, at room temperature	175 mL
1-1/2 cups	brown sugar	375 mL
2	eggs	2
1 tbsp	milk	5 mL
1 cup	chopped dates	250 mL
1 cup	chopped walnuts	250 mL
1 cup	raisins	250 mL

Store all cookies in airtight cookie jars or plastic containers to keep them fresh.

1. Preheat oven to 350° F (180° C).

2. In a bowl, combine flour, baking powder, baking soda, salt, cinnamon and nutmeg.

3. In a large bowl, beat butter and sugar together until light and fluffy. Add eggs and beat to a smooth batter. Blend in milk and mix. Stir in flour mixture, dates, walnuts and raisins.

4. Drop spoonfuls of batter on a buttered baking sheet, about 1-1/2 inches (4 cm) apart to allow for spreading.

5. Bake until lightly brown, approximately 15 to 20 minutes.

Makes about 36 cookies

Monster Cookies

1 cup	butter, at room temperature	250 mL
1-1/2 cups	packed brown sugar	375 mL
2	eggs	2
1 tsp	vanilla	5 mL
1-1/2 cups	all-purpose flour	375 mL
2-1/2 cups	rolled oats	625 mL
2 tsp	baking soda	10 mL
1 tsp	salt	5 mL
1 cup	semi-sweet chocolate chips	250 mL
1 cup	raisins	250 mL

1. Preheat oven to 300° F (150° C).

2. In a bowl, cream butter and sugar until light and fluffy. Beat in eggs and vanilla.

3. In a separate bowl, combine flour, rolled oats, baking soda and salt. Mix into egg mixture until well blended. Stir in chocolate chips and raisins.

4. Drop dough by ice-cream scoop onto well-greased baking sheets, about 3 inches (7.5 cm) apart. Flatten with the bottom of a floured glass.

5. Bake for approximately 15 to 20 minutes, or until brown on bottom. Cool.

Makes 15 cookies

Trent Rowe's Chinese Almond Cookies

A tender-crisp cookie from food writer Trent Rowe. We've added almond extract to give them even more flavour.

1 cup	rice flour	250 mL
1/2 cup	lightly packed brown sugar	125 mL
2 cups	ground blanched almonds	500 mL
1/3 cup	butter, at room temperature	75 mL
1-1/2 tsp	almond extract	7 mL
	Whole or half almonds, or halved candied cherries	

Rice flour is made from white rice and is very finely ground. It is especially useful for those on low-gluten diets.

1. Preheat oven to 350 F (180° C).

2. Sift rice flour and sugar into bowl.

3. Stir in ground almonds. Work in softened butter and almond extract, adding a little cold water if necessary (1 to 2 tbsp/15 to 25 mL) to hold dough together. Work dough with hands to a smooth ball.

4. Shape dough into small balls and place on greased baking sheets. Press an almond or cherry on top of each cookie.

5. Bake for 12 to 15 minutes, or until golden.

Makes about 36 cookies

Barbara McQuade's Pecan Dreams

Try this bite-sized, melt-in-your-mouth, cookie from Barbara McQuade of the Vancouver Sun.

2 cups	butter, at room temperature	500 mL
1/2 cup	granulated sugar	125 mL
1 tbsp	vanilla	15 mL
4 cups	all-purpose flour	1 L
1 cup	finely chopped pecans	250 mL
pinch	salt	pinch
	Pecan halves	

1. Preheat oven to 325° F (160° C).

2. In a large bowl, cream butter. Gradually add sugar and vanilla, beating until light and fluffy.

3. Add flour, nuts and salt. Mix well, then work dough with hands until all ingredients are smoothly blended.

4. Shape dough into small balls about the size of a walnut and place on baking sheets. Press a pecan half on top of each cookie.

5. Bake for 20 minutes, or just until very light golden.

Makes about 90 cookies

Sweet Marie Bars

These bars are easy to make and require no baking.

1/2 cup	corn syrup	125 mL
1 tbsp	butter	15 mL
1/2 cup	brown sugar	125 mL
1/2 cup	peanut butter	125 mL
1/2 cup	semi-sweet chocolate chips	125 mL
3/4 cup	chopped nuts	175 mL
2 cups	Rice Krispies	500 mL

Topping

2 tbsp	peanut butter	25 mL
1 cup	semi-sweet chocolate chips	250 mL

1. In a saucepan, melt together corn syrup, butter, sugar, 1/2 cup (125 mL) peanut butter and 1/2 cup (125 mL) chocolate chips. Remove from heat and stir in nuts and Rice Krispies. Press into bottom of a greased 8-inch (2 L) square baking dish.

2. In a small saucepan, heat 2 tbsp (25 mL) peanut butter and 1 cup (250 mL) chocolate chips. Spread over the base.

3. Refrigerate until firm. Cut into squares.

Makes 16 squares

Santa Cookies

These cookies are a great project for children a few days before Christmas. Decorate with coloured icings and cake decorations.

Easy kids' decoration: drizzle melted chocolate over cookies. Press Smarties into still warm dough. Cut up gumdrops and press into dough. Simple icing: combine 1 cup (250 mL) icing sugar with 1 to 2 tbsp (15 - 25 mL) warm water. Spread on cookies.

3/4 cup	granulated sugar	175 mL
1/2 cup	butter or shortening, melted	125 mL
2	eggs, well beaten	2
2 cups	all-purpose flour	500 mL
1 tsp	cream of tartar	5 mL
1/2 tsp	baking soda	2 mL
1/2 tsp	salt	2 mL
1 tsp	vanilla	5 mL

1. In a large mixing bowl, beat sugar, butter and eggs together until combined.

2. In a separate bowl, combine flour, cream of tartar, baking soda and salt. Beat into the egg mixture. Add vanilla and mix well.

3. Chill dough for about 30 minutes so that it can be easily handled.

4. Preheat oven to 375° F (190° C).

5. Roll dough to 1/8-inch (3 mm) thickness and cut into Santa shapes with a cookie cutter.

6. Place cookies on a greased baking sheet 2 inches (5 cm) apart.

7. Bake for 5 to 8 minutes, or until light brown.

Makes 36 cookies

Shelley Peterson's Chocolate Chip-Raisin Cookies

Shelley Peterson often whips together a batch of these cookies for her children after school.

Cookies will be crisper if they are removed to racks to cool. If they are cooled on the baking sheets, they will remain chewier.

1/2 cup	butter, at room temperature	125 mL
1/2 cup	packed brown sugar	125 mL
1/4 cup	granulated sugar	50 mL
1	egg	1
1 tsp	vanilla	5 mL
1 cup	all-purpose flour	250 mL
1/2 tsp	baking soda	2 mL
1/2 tsp	salt	2 mL
1 cup	semi-sweet chocolate chips	250 mL
1 cup	raisins	250 mL

1. Preheat oven to 375° F (190° C).

2. In a large bowl, cream together butter and sugars. Beat in egg and vanilla.

3. In a separate bowl, combine flour, baking soda and salt. Gradually blend into the creamed mixture.

4. Stir in chocolate chips and raisins.

5. Drop from a spoon onto ungreased baking sheets, about 1-1/2 inches (4 cm) apart.

6. Bake for 10 to 12 minutes, or until firm. Cool on a wire rack.

Makes 12 large cookies

Raisin Chews

2	eggs	2
1 cup	granulated sugar	250 mL
3/4 cup	all-purpose flour	175 mL
1/2 tsp	baking powder	2 mL
1/2 tsp	salt	2 mL
1 cup	grated coconut	250 mL
1 cup	chopped raisins	250 mL
1-1/2 cups	chopped nuts	375 mL

1. Preheat oven to 350° F (180° C).

2. In a large bowl, beat eggs. Add sugar and beat well.

3. In a separate bowl, combine flour, baking powder and salt. Blend into first mixture.

4. Stir in coconut, raisins and nuts. Mix and press into a greased 9-inch (2.5 L) square baking dish.

5. Bake for 25 minutes until firm. Let cool and cut into squares.

Makes 16 squares

Chocolate Bars

A very easy chocolate square.

First Layer

1/4 cup	cocoa	50 mL
3 tbsp	granulated sugar	45 mL
3/4 cup	all-purpose flour	175 mL
1/2 cup	butter	125 mL

Second Layer

2	eggs	2
1-1/4 cups	brown sugar	300 mL
3 tbsp	all-purpose flour	45 mL
1/4 tsp	salt	1 mL
1 tsp	baking powder	5 mL
1/2 cup	chopped nuts	125 mL
1/2 cup	grated coconut	125 mL
1 tsp	vanilla	5 mL

1. Preheat oven to 350° F (180° C).

2. In a bowl, combine cocoa, sugar and flour. Cut in butter until mixture is crumbly. Pat into a greased 9-inch (2.5 L) square baking dish. Bake for 15 minutes. Cool slightly.

3. In a bowl, blend together all ingredients for second layer. Pour over first layer. Bake for about 20 minutes, or until firm. Cut into squares when cool.

Makes 20 squares

Quickie Candy

1/2 cup	peanut butter	125 mL
1/2 cup	skim milk powder	125 mL
1/2 cup	wheat germ	125 mL
1/2 cup	liquid honey	125 mL
2 tbsp	sesame seeds or chopped peanuts	25 mL

1. In a large bowl, mix together all ingredients.

2. Shape mixture into 1-inch (2.5 cm) balls. Refrigerate until needed.

Makes about 24 balls

Peanut Butter Balls

For a special occasion, peel bananas and wrap them in foil. When frozen, unwrap and dip the bananas in melted chocolate.

2 cups	crunchy peanut butter	500 mL
2 cups	icing sugar	500 mL
2 cups	Rice Krispies	500 mL
8 oz	semi-sweet chocolate	250 g
2 tbsp	butter	25 mL

1. In a large bowl, combine peanut butter, sugar and Rice Krispies. Shape into 1-inch (2.5 cm) balls. Put in freezer for 2 hours.

2. In a saucepan, melt chocolate and butter over low heat. Using toothpicks, dip balls into chocolate mixture. Dry on waxed paper.

Makes 48 balls

Brown Sugar Fudge

*Beat the fudge until it is creamy and just becoming slightly granular.
It takes a little practice to get the consistency just right, but the
flavour is always great!*

1 cup	butter	250 mL
2 lb	brown sugar	1 kg
1	10-oz (284 mL) can evaporated milk	1

Store the candy in an airtight container – it will become even softer and creamier.

1. Place ingredients in a saucepan on medium heat. Cook until mixture comes to a boil, stirring frequently. Boil and stir for about 45 minutes, until very thick.

2. Remove mixture from heat and pour into mixing bowl. Beat at medium speed for 2 to 3 minutes. As soon as mixture begins to stiffen, pour immediately into a greased 8-inch (2 L) square baking dish.

3. Place dish in sink in a shallow pool of cold water and, with a wooden spoon, continue beating for 5 minutes, until thick. Cut fudge into squares while still warm.

Makes about 30 squares

Caramel Corn

Make your own caramel corn; it's better and fresher than the commercial kind.

Cream of tartar: a fine white powder that will help to increase the volume of egg whites. The acid reacts with the protein to stabilize them, making them less likely to collapse.

12 cups	popped popcorn	3 L
1-1/2 cups	pecans (optional)	375 mL
2 cups	lightly packed brown sugar	500 mL
1/2 cup	corn syrup	125 mL
1 cup	butter	250 mL
1/4 tsp	cream of tartar	1 mL
1 tsp	salt	5 mL
1 tsp	baking soda	5 mL

1. Preheat oven to 250° F (120° C).

2. Place popcorn and pecans in large buttered roasting pan. Keep warm in oven.

3. In a large saucepan, combine brown sugar, corn syrup, butter, cream of tartar and salt. Bring to a boil and stir constantly until mixture reaches 260° F (126° C) on candy thermometer.

4. Remove from heat and stir in baking soda quickly but thoroughly. Pour syrup mixture over popcorn. Stir gently until well coated.

5. Reduce oven temperature to 200° F (90° C). Bake popcorn for 1 hour, stirring 2 or 3 times.

6. Turn out onto a lightly buttered counter. Allow to cool before breaking into pieces.

Makes about 12 cups (3 L)

INDEX